AFRICA'S GREAT LAKES REGION: A SECURITY, POLITICAL, AND HUMANITARIAN CHALLENGE

HEARING

BEFORE THE

SUBCOMMITTEE ON AFRICA, GLOBAL HEALTH, GLOBAL HUMAN RIGHTS, AND INTERNATIONAL ORGANIZATIONS

OF THE

COMMITTEE ON FOREIGN AFFAIRS HOUSE OF REPRESENTATIVES

ONE HUNDRED FOURTEENTH CONGRESS

FIRST SESSION

OCTOBER 22, 2015

Serial No. 114–107

Printed for the use of the Committee on Foreign Affairs

Available via the World Wide Web: http://www.foreignaffairs.house.gov/ or http://www.gpo.gov/fdsys/

U.S. GOVERNMENT PUBLISHING OFFICE

97–267PDF   WASHINGTON : 2015

For sale by the Superintendent of Documents, U.S. Government Publishing Office
Internet: bookstore.gpo.gov   Phone: toll free (866) 512–1800; DC area (202) 512–1800
Fax: (202) 512–2104   Mail: Stop IDCC, Washington, DC 20402–0001

COMMITTEE ON FOREIGN AFFAIRS

EDWARD R. ROYCE, California, *Chairman*

CHRISTOPHER H. SMITH, New Jersey
ILEANA ROS-LEHTINEN, Florida
DANA ROHRABACHER, California
STEVE CHABOT, Ohio
JOE WILSON, South Carolina
MICHAEL T. McCAUL, Texas
TED POE, Texas
MATT SALMON, Arizona
DARRELL E. ISSA, California
TOM MARINO, Pennsylvania
JEFF DUNCAN, South Carolina
MO BROOKS, Alabama
PAUL COOK, California
RANDY K. WEBER SR., Texas
SCOTT PERRY, Pennsylvania
RON DeSANTIS, Florida
MARK MEADOWS, North Carolina
TED S. YOHO, Florida
CURT CLAWSON, Florida
SCOTT DesJARLAIS, Tennessee
REID J. RIBBLE, Wisconsin
DAVID A. TROTT, Michigan
LEE M. ZELDIN, New York
DANIEL DONOVAN, New York

ELIOT L. ENGEL, New York
BRAD SHERMAN, California
GREGORY W. MEEKS, New York
ALBIO SIRES, New Jersey
GERALD E. CONNOLLY, Virginia
THEODORE E. DEUTCH, Florida
BRIAN HIGGINS, New York
KAREN BASS, California
WILLIAM KEATING, Massachusetts
DAVID CICILLINE, Rhode Island
ALAN GRAYSON, Florida
AMI BERA, California
ALAN S. LOWENTHAL, California
GRACE MENG, New York
LOIS FRANKEL, Florida
TULSI GABBARD, Hawaii
JOAQUIN CASTRO, Texas
ROBIN L. KELLY, Illinois
BRENDAN F. BOYLE, Pennsylvania

AMY PORTER, *Chief of Staff*   THOMAS SHEEHY, *Staff Director*

JASON STEINBAUM, *Democratic Staff Director*

————

SUBCOMMITTEE ON AFRICA, GLOBAL HEALTH, GLOBAL HUMAN RIGHTS, AND INTERNATIONAL ORGANIZATIONS

CHRISTOPHER H. SMITH, New Jersey, *Chairman*

MARK MEADOWS, North Carolina
CURT CLAWSON, Florida
SCOTT DesJARLAIS, Tennessee
DANIEL DONOVAN, New York

KAREN BASS, California
DAVID CICILLINE, Rhode Island
AMI BERA, California

CONTENTS

AFRICA'S GREAT LAKES REGION: A SECURITY, POLITICAL, AND HUMANITARIAN CHALLENGE

THURSDAY, OCTOBER 22, 2015

House of Representatives,
Subcommittee on Africa, Global Health,
Global Human Rights, and International Organizations,
Committee on Foreign Affairs,
Washington, DC.

The subcommittee met, pursuant to notice, at 2:03 p.m., in room 2200 Rayburn House Office Building, Hon. Christopher H. Smith (chairman of the subcommittee) presiding.

Mr. SMITH. The subcommittee will come to order and thank you to our very highly distinguished witnesses for being here and for taking the time to provide your insights and counsel to this subcommittee.

Ladies and gentlemen, to state that the Great Lakes region of Africa is troubled would be an understatement. Burundi is experiencing continued turmoil due to a recent contentious election. The Democratic Republic of the Congo, or DRC, has had some level of conflict since the late 1990s. The Lord's Resistance Army, also known as the LRA, has plagued several of these countries. Alleged plundering of DRC resources by Rwanda and Uganda has never been fully resolved. Nations in the region have been preoccupied in the last 2 years with resolving the South Sudanese Civil War.

Definitions vary, but the Great Lakes region, as defined by the U.S. Department of State, comprises Burundi, DRC, Rwanda, and Uganda. The region is among the most densely populated in Africa, especially around Lake Victoria, and enjoys rich agricultural potential, water resources, minerals, and wildlife. However, political instability, conflict, humanitarian crises, and lack of development remain key challenges.

These four countries are the purview of the U.S. Special Envoy to the Great Lakes, Tom Perriello, who we are delighted to have here today, a former Member of the House and a former member of the committee I served on for years and that is the Veterans Affairs Committee. So Tom, thank you for being here.

We also have Assistant Secretary of State for African Affairs, an expert in the field, Linda Thomas-Greenfield, who has spent a great deal of her time in office dealing with the Great Lakes and a great deal of time on the road. It has been hard to get you up here, but I know, as you said just a moment ago, you have been

(1)

spending 3 weeks out of four on the road and that is very commendable on your part to spend so much time working on these
issues.

Today's hearing offers an opportunity to hear from these top administration officials, not only about continuing U.S. efforts to ex-
tinguish the LRA threat, but also the administration's work with
governments in the region on issues such as peace building, governance, and adherence to internationally recognized human rights
and democracy.

In our subcommittee hearings over the last 3 years, we have un-
covered numerous troubling situations. Even with the supposed
end of the operations by M23 militia, an issue in DRC, in late
2013, there are several other militias still causing instability in the
region. The Kabila government in the DRC reportedly is using a
ban on completing foreign adoptions as leverage to ward off actions
to prevent him from prolonging in his rule, despite a constitutional
bar to any reelection bid.

The Burundian President's decision to run for a third term,
which some Burundians and outside observers viewed as a violation of a landmark peace agreement and arguably the Constitution
of Burundi, has led to a political crisis and heightened concerns
about regional stability.

Human rights abuses in Rwanda were found to be targeted toward real or perceived political opponents prior to 2012, but after
2012, such abuses were seen as more random, expanding the targets of the regime. Major Robert Higiro, a retired Rwandan military officer, told our subcommittee on May 20th about his solicita-
tion by the Rwandan intelligence chief to kill high-level defectors.
He turned against the government and informed the targets who
asked him to record the offer. He did, and the recording was vali-
dated by the Globe and Mail in Canada and the British Broad-
casting Corporation, the BBC. The State Department has not only
found the allegation to be credible but warned Major Higiro to
leave Belgium where his life was in danger.

Although LRA killings have diminished in the past few years,
kidnappings by the group have risen as it operates in smaller, scat-
tered cells using more adults as temporary labor. One witness at
our hearing last month said an end to the U.S. support for the
counter-LRA effort would be ''devastating,'' I believe the administration will continue that counter-LRA effort and that is encour-
aging.

We have heard of the difficulties of addressing issues in this
troubled region of Africa by both governments and private witnesses over the last few years, however, the fates of these countries
are interconnected and our policies need to take that into account.

I would like to yield to Mr. Cicilline for any opening comments
he might have.

Mr. CICILLINE. Thank you, Mr. Chairman. And thank you for
calling this hearing today and to our distinguished witnesses for
being here to share your experiences and recommendations for U.S.
policy toward this region.

When I think of the Great Lakes region in Africa what so often
comes to mind is the incredible conflict and suffering that the region has experienced in recent decades. The wars in Burundi and

DRC and genocide in Rwanda unleash true horrors upon the population. But despite their troubled past, the countries of the Great Lakes region, Burundi, the Democratic Republic of the Congo, Rwanda, and Uganda have made some progress. Peace accords restored a semblance of stability to Burundi and the DRC. Rwanda has become an example in terms of economic development of the region. Uganda has experienced relative peace and stability.

I recently visited Rwanda and had the opportunity to see some of this progress first-hand; however, there remain great challenges to regional stability and for the forward progress of these countries. Public health issues, violence against women, HIV/AIDS, and food security remain challenges throughout the region. Moreover, leaders in Burundi, DRC, and Rwanda have indicated reluctance to allow for peaceful transitions of power. Burundi President Pierre Nkurunziza's decision to run for a third term in contravention of the Arusha Accords is very troubling as are indications that the Presidents of the DRC and Rwanda may attempt to circumvent term limits in their own countries. President Museveni has ruled Uganda since 1986.

I firmly believe that further economic development of these countries and improvements in their health, safety, and food security will be directly tied to their acceptance of free and fair democratic process.

I look forward to hearing from our witnesses today as to how Congress can encourage these countries to maintain a democratic trajectory. And with that, I yield back and thank you, Mr. Chairman.

Mr. SMITH. I would like to yield to Mark Meadows.

Mr. MEADOWS. Thank you, Mr. Chairman. Thank you for continuing to make humanitarian relief a focus of this subcommittee on a regular basis and for me, it is very gratifying to have both of you here to testify today. We look forward to hearing not only your expert testimony, but how we can go beyond a hearing and make an impact in countries that most Americans would have a hard time finding on a map.

We see the devastation. We hear the stories, but they are headlines and they are far away. And we need to do a better job as Members of Congress, but we also need to do a better job of highlighting those areas where we can make a difference. So I look forward to hearing from both of you on perhaps two things that we are doing well, but two things that we need drastic improvement on and that way we can have actionable items. And with that, I will yield back, Mr. Chairman.

Mr. SMITH. Thank you very much, Mr. Meadows. I would like to introduce our two distinguished witnesses, beginning first with Ambassador Linda Thomas-Greenfield, a member of the career Foreign Service who was sworn in on August 6, 2013 as the Assistant Secretary for African Affairs. Prior to assuming her current position, she led a team of about 400 employees who carried out personnel functions for the State Department's 70,000 strong work force.

Since beginning her Foreign Service career in 1982, I note parenthetically, a year after I came to Congress, she has risen through the ranks to the Minister Counselor level, serving in Jamaica, Nigeria, The Gambia, Kenya, Pakistan, and at the U.S. Mission to the United Nations, and most recently as Ambassador to Liberia where she served from 2008 to 2012.

Then we will hear from the Honorable Thomas Perriello, Special Envoy for the Great Lakes Region of Africa. He previously served as Special Representative for the Quadrennial Diplomacy and Development Review and also served as a Congressman from Virginia. And I would note also that he served on the House Committee on Veterans' Affairs and I thank him for that service. I served on that committee as well. He was also a Special Advisor to the Prosecutor of the Special Court for Sierra Leone, an extremely effective court that was led by David Crane, as we all know, and ultimately secured a major conviction and that was of Charles Taylor, who got 50 years for the atrocities that he unleashed upon the people in Sierra Leone and Liberia.

He has also served as CEO of the Center for American Progress Action. He has worked and conducted research in a dozen countries and taught courses on transitional justice at the University of Virginia's School of Law and the University of Sierra Leone.

Outside of government, Mr. Perriello has co-founded and managed justice entrepreneurship platforms and faith-based organizations advancing human rights, poverty reduction, and sustainability.

Madam Ambassador, the floor is yours.

STATEMENT OF THE HONORABLE LINDA THOMAS–GREEN-FIELD, ASSISTANT SECRETARY, BUREAU OF AFRICAN AFFAIRS, U.S. DEPARTMENT OF STATE

Ambassador THOMAS-GREENFIELD. Thank you very much, Chairman Smith and thanks to the other members of the subcommittee for the opportunity to testify today on the many challenges facing the central African region. I am honored to testify here today with Special Envoy to the Great Lakes Region of Africa, Tom Perriello, one of your former colleagues.

The Department and the Bureau of African Affairs, in particular, greatly appreciates the bipartisan support we continue to receive for our work, for our Embassies, and for our people who spend every single day striving to promote our national security, foreign policy, and economic interests on the continent of Africa.

In the central African region, particularly in the countries of Rwanda, Burundi, the Democratic Republic of the Congo (DRC), the Republic of Congo, our efforts to strengthen democratic institutions, spur economic growth, advance peace and security, and promote opportunity and development have borne fruit. However, the progress made in this region is fragile and it is at great risk, as you both described in your remarks. In fact, this is the region that I am most concerned about as it is way out of step of the progression that the rest of continent is making.

I know that you are interested in our continuing efforts to combat the Lord's Resistance Army, also known as the LRA, and I am pleased to report that we actually have had some good success there, in fact, great success working through our regional partners, notably Uganda and the African Union. The Central African Republic, despite intense conflicts in that country, the Democratic Republic of the Congo with its political issues, South Sudan at war with itself, all have actively provided assistance to us in countering the LRA. Over 270 people have either defected, escaped, or been released since 2012. Four of the five top commanders are in The Hague. The number of people killed by the LRA has dropped by 90 percent since 2010 when 365 were killed and we have had 19 killed since June 30, 2015. Even that is too many, but it is a significant decrease.

These numbers make it clear that our strategy is working, but Joseph Kony is still commanding the remnants of the LRA and until he is brought to justice we remain committed to finishing the work that we have started.

President Obama's July speech to the African Union in Addis Ababa where he addressed the critical issue of democratic transition including term limits, respect for constitutions, and the peaceful transfer of leadership, has resonated resoundingly on the continent. The core principles the President elaborated are the cornerstone of our engagement with leaders whose time in office should be coming to an end. And note that I said ''should.'' Over the next 2 years, each of the countries in this region has faced or will face the opportunity to realize a true democratic transfer of power. Yet, in each of these countries, that agreed-upon process is in doubt. The leaders of these nations have been making fateful decisions whether or not to abide by their previous commitments, respect the rule of law and their constitutions, and responsibly build a foundation of peaceful, elected, democratic leadership and transition.

In Burundi, President Nkurunziza's pursuit of a third term caused the current volatile political crisis. Prevailing circumstances have forced over 200,000 Burundians to flee into neighboring countries since April and many of those attempting to flee have reported violent confrontations by party militias and police. Special Envoy Perriello just returned from the region and will provide more context on our current efforts there.

While the Republic of Congo is outside our definition of the Great Lakes region, it impacts it and is affected by similar situations as elsewhere in the region. President Sassou Nguesso's decision to call for a popular referendum on a proposed new constitution is deeply troubling and has created a volatile situation that could spiral beyond the government's control with tragic results. And as I speak today, the current situation in the country is very, very tense.

I now turn to circumstances across the Congo River in the Democratic Republic of the Congo. Before I get into the electoral and security situations I would like to assure you, the Members of Congress, and any of your constituents who are anxiously waiting to bring their adopted children home, that we remain closely engaged with DRC officials at the highest levels to lift the ban on exit permits for the hundreds of legally-adopted children who are unable to join their new families and we will not cease in our efforts until all of these cases are resolved.

On the political front, we remain deeply concerned by the situation in DRC. President Kabila's final term is due to end in December 2016. Efforts by the President to amend the constitution or guarantee electoral delays have been vigorously resisted, even by some of his own majority in the DRC Parliament and certainly by his citizens. Tom has also just concluded a visit from that country and he will go into more details on our analysis and our approach to the situation, but I must note that at this time I don't see that DRC is yet at a precipice. President Kabila faces a choice. He can establish a tradition of peaceful transition of power for his country or he can set back the significant progress that he himself has made during his tenure by trying to stay in office beyond his term.

Finally, on Rwanda, the United States has been a strong partner with Rwanda. While it has been making significant and commendable strides in spurring economic growth and promoting development following the devastating 1994 genocide, we continue to encourage Rwanda to demonstrate significantly greater respect for human rights and democratic principles. Thus, I have to admit we were very disappointed when the Rwandan Government established a constitutional reform commission that has recommended removing executive term limits that would permit President Kagame to seek a third term in 2017 and we have urged him against this.

Chairman Smith and members of the subcommittee, I want to thank you again for holding this hearing and giving us the opportunity to discuss our extensive engagement in the region. I hope that the information that we share with you today, as well as with the audience here, is helpful. I look forward to answering all of your questions as I know Tom will.

[The prepared statement of Ambassador Thomas-Greenfield follows:]

Testimony of Assistant Secretary Linda Thomas-Greenfield

Bureau of African Affairs, U.S. Department of State

House Foreign Affairs Committee

Subcommittee on African Affairs

October 22, 2015

Thank you very much Chairman Smith, Ranking Member Bass, and other Members of the Committee for the opportunity to testify today on the diverse challenges facing the Central African region. I am honored to testify today with Special Envoy to the Great Lakes Region of Africa Tom Perriello.

The Department and the Bureau of African Affairs in particular greatly appreciate the bipartisan support we continue to receive for our work, our embassies, and our people who spend every day striving to promote U.S. national security, foreign policy, and economic interests on the African continent.

It has been over three years since the U.S. Government began implementing the President's four-pillar strategy toward sub-Saharan Africa. In the Central African region, particularly in the countries of Rwanda, Burundi, the Democratic Republic of the Congo, and the Republic of the Congo, our efforts to strengthen democratic institutions, spur economic growth, advance peace and security, and promote opportunity and development have seen some success and have been met with some setbacks. The progress made in the region is fragile and is at great risk; in fact, this is the region that I am the most concerned about, as it is out of step with the progression of the rest of the continent. President Obama's July speech to the African Union in Addis Ababa, in which he addressed the critical issue of democratic transition -- including term limits, respect for constitutions, and the peaceful transfer of leadership -- resonated resoundingly across the region. The core principles the President elaborated are the cornerstone of our engagement with leaders who, like President Obama, are facing an end to their time in office according to their own constitutions.

Beginning this past spring and summer and continuing over the next two years, each of the countries in this region has faced or will face the opportunity to realize a true democratic transfer of power. Yet in each of these situations, that agreed-upon process is in doubt. The leaders of these nations have been making fateful decisions whether or not to abide by their previous commitments, respect the rule of law, and responsibly build a foundation of peaceful, elected, democratic leadership and stewardship. And while the challenges facing these countries in this regard are similar, each country's unique history and current socioeconomic reality lend themselves to different approaches for achieving the desired outcome.

Burundi

President Pierre Nkurunziza's ultimate decision to stand for a third presidential term in Burundi was preceded by months of increasingly harsh repression, intimidation, and violence towards legitimate political opposition, independent media, and anyone within his own party who dissented against this plan. Nkurunziza's pursuit of a third term caused the current volatile crisis. This move was a clear violation of the terms of the Arusha Agreement that led to the end of the Burundian Civil War and became the foundation for governance, peace and security. The elections, held in late July, were widely viewed as not fair, not free, and not transparent. The ruling party's youth wing—the *Imbonerakure*—has been armed and has used extreme violence with impunity. We have also been concerned that the government has taken no action to hold accountable members of the Burundian police and internal intelligence services, who have been credibly alleged to have committed egregious human rights abuses. There are reports of widespread, systematic corruption in government finances to serve the interests of the ruling party and individuals within it. Prevailing circumstances have forced over 200,000 Burundians to flee into neighboring countries since April. Many of those attempting to flee have reported violent confrontations by party militias and police while en route.

The United States continues to urge all Burundian stakeholders to undertake a comprehensive and inclusive dialogue as the best route to finding consensus on a peaceful path forward that preserves the Arusha Agreement, restores stability, and prevents mass atrocities. We support the African Union's strong October 17 statement, calling for EAC mediation efforts and reiterating the immediate need for a genuine and inclusive dialogue. We have consistently condemned violent acts from any quarter – including the attempt to unlawfully seize power in May, and the brutal suppression of protests by security services – and we will continue to do so. Since the beginning of 2014 the Secretary, previous Special Envoy Feingold, Ambassador Power, Bureau of Democracy, Human Rights, and Labor Assistant Secretary Malinowski, and I have met with President Nkurunziza at different times to emphasize the importance of respecting the principles of the Arusha Agreement, and emphasizing the connection between good governance and the gains in stability Burundi had made since 2005. We continue to engage all Burundian stakeholders and regional leaders in support of the East African Community's efforts to mediate the crisis with the full inclusion of both the governing party and peaceful representatives of the broad Burundian political opposition and even broader civil society.

Though we do not provide direct budget assistance to the Government of Burundi, we do undertake activities that protect vulnerable populations, for example: by supporting critical health services and mitigating conflict. Our assistance promotes reconciliation and dialogue among youth. We also provide aid that reduces malnutrition among children and improves maternal healthcare.

Ongoing programs managed by the Bureau of Conflict and Stabilization Operations engage at-risk youth in conflict prevention and mediation training, facilitate community-level efforts to deescalate violence, and support inclusive political dialogue efforts. In FY 2015, the U.S. government also provided roughly $34 million in assistance for HIV/AIDS and malaria prevention and treatment, as well as maternal and child healthcare services. We have suspended assistance to Burundi's police forces given their violent suppression of demonstrations and disturbing allegations of their involvement in extrajudicial killings and torture, and we have significantly curtailed assistance to the military, continuing only some aspects of assistance to units currently conducting regional peacekeeping missions in Somalia and the Central African Republic as part of our support for those multilateral missions.

Nkurunziza's grip on power has come at a steep price to the citizens of Burundi, but we are committed to supporting the people of Burundi to achieve a just and lasting peace based on democratic principles, and will continue to work with all stakeholders to make that happen.

Republic of Congo

While the Republic of Congo (RoC) is outside of our definition of the Great Lakes region, it impacts upon and is affected by similar situations in the region. On October 7, President Denis Sassou N'Guesso called for a popular referendum on October 25 to vote on a proposed new constitution that would overcome existing age and immutable term limits, and would allow him to run again for up to three more terms of five years each. This decision is deeply troubling, especially as the proposed new constitution was developed behind closed doors, with little to no input from the broader body politic or civil society. Congolese citizens will have had less than two weeks to review the document and no opportunity for comment other than to cast an up or down vote. The vote is scheduled to occur prior to the implementation of agreed-upon improvements to electoral governance that would build confidence and improve the credibility of results at the polls. This has created a volatile situation where even a small spark could cause the situation to spiral beyond the government's control with tragic results, and we have already seen violence erupting there this week.

The RoC has made progress in recent years, developing the country's infrastructure, and increasing security cooperation in the Gulf of Guinea and on the neighboring Central African Republic. However, transitioning to democracy and a free market economy remains a challenge. The ruling party firmly controls all mechanisms of government; human rights abuses persist; the judiciary is weak; unemployment is at 40 percent; the economy is overly reliant on falling oil revenues; government finances are not entirely transparent; and the challenging business climate inhibits both domestic entrepreneurship and foreign investment. Congolese citizens recognize that their standard of living has not significantly improved despite the considerable rebuilding of physical infrastructure since the 1997-2003 civil war and the substantial government oil revenues that nominally make the RoC a lower middle-income country.

While we do not provide direct budget support to its government, the United States and the RoC have enjoyed increasingly close relations over the last ten years, cooperating on issues ranging from peacekeeper training to environmentalism and health awareness to a school feeding program, among others. We continue to fund health and education programs, while recognizing that our bilateral relationship with RoC will depend in part on the outcome of the upcoming electoral season.

The current situation in Brazzaville is tense, and our Ambassador there, Stephanie Sullivan, is working tirelessly to help stem violence. She meets frequently with Congolese government and opposition figures to advocate for freedom of peaceful expression and assembly and urge restraint, while simultaneously reiterating our position against constitutional change that allows term-limited incumbents to remain in power. Ambassador Sullivan also consults with her counterparts from other like-minded diplomatic missions and international and non-governmental organizations and figures in Brazzaville to bring the parties together.

We will continue both in public and in private to articulate our position on term limits and democratic transition with senior government ROC officials. The State Department will also continue to emphasize to Congolese government officials that regular, peaceful, democratic leadership transitions provide a dynamic and healthy mechanism for citizens to hold political leaders accountable for their governance and foster long-term stability. No democracy is served when its leaders alter national constitutions for personal or political gain.

Democratic Republic of the Congo

I'll now turn to circumstances across the Congo River in the Democratic Republic of the Congo (DRC). Before I get into the electoral and security situations, however, I'd like to take a moment to explain our position on an issue that has become a significant wedge in our bilateral relations: the continued suspension of exit permits for internationally adopted children. In September 2013, the Congolese government suspended the issuance of exit permits for internationally adopted children after noting an increase in adoption applications from foreigners. The Congolese government cited concerns about possible corruption within its adoption process. As you know, despite the exit permit ban, DRC courts have continued to issue adoption decrees.

Over the past two years, U.S. officials have increasingly engaged with DRC officials at many levels to lift the ban for the hundreds of legally adopted children unable to join their new families. President Obama called President Joseph Kabila to urge him to action. Secretary Kerry has pressed President Kabila to resolve this matter on several occasions. Assistant Secretary of State for Consular Affairs Michele Bond traveled to the DRC in March and August, and Bureau of African Affairs Deputy Assistant Secretary Stuart Symington also engaged government officials there in August. Dr. Jill Biden sent a letter to President Kabila's sister, Jaynet Kabila, in September urging her to consider the humanitarian implications for the children. Our efforts are also being matched with similar high-level engagement by our donor partners whose citizens have adopted children in the DRC. We are grateful that many of you in Congress have made this issue a continuing priority.

Nevertheless, the DRC government has failed to resolve this issue despite many repeated promises over the past 24 plus months to do so. As a result, approximately 400 children legally adopted by U.S. citizens—along with an additional 700 adopted by families from other countries—wait to be united with their loving families. We have also learned that several legally adopted children have died in the DRC while waiting to be united with their adoptive families.

The Department believes the Congolese government should be reminded repeatedly of the importance of immediately releasing all 1,100 children with finalized adoptions. During the United Nations General Assembly meetings last month in New York, Special Envoy Perriello and I once again raised the plight of these children with DRC Foreign Minister Tshibanda and the Congolese delegation. Tshibanda and other Congolese officials, including the new DRC Ambassador to the United States, promised a resolution "soon." I want to assure you —Members of Congress and your constituents who anxiously wait to bring their children home—this issue remains a priority for the Department. And we will not relent in our efforts until all of these cases are resolved.

The White House's announcement yesterday of the continuation of the declaration of a national emergency with respect to the Democratic Republic of the Congo illustrates that on the political front we remain deeply concerned by the situation there. The DRC has slowly emerged from the 1996-2003 era of what many have called Africa's World War, which saw over 5.8 million civilians killed by war and related disease. In 2006 and 2011, Congolese citizens voted in the first democratic elections the country had seen since its independence in 1960. The 2006 elections, while generally lauded as a success, were heavily supported by the international community with funding and logistical support. While they happened on time, the subsequent 2011 elections were criticized as seriously flawed and lacking in transparency. These two electoral cycles ushered in significant political, economic, and social progress including the flourishing of a vibrant civil society, the construction of urban infrastructure, and GDP growth rates upwards of nine percent per year.

The DRC's 2006 constitution, which represents to many Congolese the completion of a process that brought much-needed peace, provides for the

President to serve two consecutive five-year terms. President Kabila's final term is due to end in December 2016. Efforts by the president's parliamentary alliance thus far to amend the constitution or guarantee electoral delay have been vigorously resisted by the opposition, including some in the presidential majority alliance, and the citizenry.

Tom has just concluded a visit there and will go into more detail on our analysis and approach to the situation, but I must note that, at this time, the DRC is not yet at the precipice. There is still time to give priority to holding national elections by the end of 2016. President Kabila faces a choice to solidify his legacy as the first democratically elected President in the DRC's history to establish a tradition of peaceful transition of power; or, he can choose to stay in office, undermining his legacy and ushering an era of instability that will significantly set back the significant progress that has been made during his tenure. It is our hope that he chooses wisely.

The United States has and continues to use the four-pillar approach towards the DRC. In the programs we fund, the policies we support, and the messages we deliver to all actors in the DRC, including President Kabila, we promote accountable, transparent, responsive governance that supports justice and respect for human rights. We seek to strengthen political parties, build rule of law, demand justice and accountability for human rights violations and mass atrocities, promote voter and civic education, provide technical electoral assistance, and build knowledge about the U.S.-DRC relationship through public diplomacy programs. We have tied the DRC's eligibility for renewed benefits under the African Growth and Opportunity Act (AGOA) to the holding of free, fair, and on-time national elections to promote an enabling environment for trade and investment. We continue to engage with the government, UN agencies, and civil society to ensure civilian protection in the likely event of instability and to bring to justice those who direct and perpetrate violence against civilians. It is our grim assessment that the risk of mass atrocities in the DRC will sharply increase if national elections do not take place on time or if President Kabila extends his mandate. We urge and support the resumption of cooperation between the UN Mission in the DRC (MONUSCO) and the DRC government. Such cooperation would be aimed at protecting civilians and, as promised since this time last year, taking on and eliminating the Democratic Forces for the Liberation of Rwanda (FDLR) and other illegal armed groups that continue to operate and wreak havoc across the east of the country, and which might take advantage of any potential political crisis to expand their power through murder, rape, and pillage. Only with the establishment of sustainable peace and stability will we be able to realize the full benefits of our substantial support to Congolese Government efforts in promoting the welfare of Congolese citizens, especially in the areas of health and education.

Rwanda

The United States has been a strong partner with Rwanda as it continues rebuilding its political, economic, and social structures following the devastating 1994 genocide. While Rwanda has made significant and commendable strides in spurring economic growth and promoting development, we continue to encourage the government to play a constructive role in the region and demonstrate significantly greater respect for human rights and democratic principles.

Rwanda has become a model of inclusive economic growth and a world leader in leveraging development assistance into socioeconomic gains for the vast majority of its people. The United States and Rwanda share the belief that trade, investment, technological development, and market forces are keys to Rwanda's long-term economic development. We have been proud to partner with Rwanda over the past decade as its economy has grown at an average of over seven per cent per year, as its infant and child mortality rates have been halved, and as HIV and malaria rates have been reduced dramatically with help from the President's Emergency Fund for AIDS Relief (PEPFAR) and the President's Malaria Initiative (PMI), respectively. We have recognized Rwanda's leading role in peacekeeping —it is the fifth largest contributor of troops in the world despite its small size and population—by designating it as a priority partner in President Obama's Africa Peacekeeping Rapid Response Partnership. At the same time, we continue to encourage Rwanda to play a constructive role in the Great Lakes region, and were pleased when Rwanda ended its support to the M23 rebellion in eastern DRC and supported the Nairobi declarations that ended that conflict. We urge Rwanda to continue to follow a policy of constructive diplomatic engagement, rather than sponsoring armed groups, during a period where some of its neighbors face instability and violence, as in Burundi.

The 2017 presidential election is a tremendous opportunity for President Kagame to cement his legacy as a leader who put in place the institutions and systems to sustain his country's development and security well into the future, and who executed an historic peaceful transition of power in accordance with his country's constitution. Thus, we were disappointed when the Rwandan government established a Constitutional Reform Commission that has recommended removing executive term limits, thereby permitting President Paul Kagame to seek a third term in 2017, if he so chooses. We have conveyed to the Rwandan government, both in public and private, that while we respect the ability of any parliament to pass legislation that reflects the will of the people, we continue to firmly support the principle of democratic transitions of power in all countries through free, fair, and credible elections, held in accordance with existing constitutional provisions on term limits and to encourage President Kagame not to seek a third term. President Kagame has repeatedly stated his commitment to respecting constitutional term limits and to mentoring a generation of leaders able to sustain Rwanda's growth and security, which we would welcome and support.

Uganda

Uganda will also be among the many African countries holding elections next year. As the campaign season begins in November, the United States will continue to encourage a free, fair, and transparent process. Uganda's leaders, security forces, political candidates, and media all have a responsibility to foster an environment in which all Ugandans can express their diverse views in peace, free of violence and intimidation.

Countering the Lord's Resistance Army

With regard to the ongoing efforts to help end the threat posed by the Lord's Resistance Army (LRA), I am pleased to report there has been great success through our regional partners, Uganda, Central African Republic (CAR), the Democratic Republic of the Congo (DRC), and South Sudan. However, since its leader, Joseph Kony, remains at large, the LRA will continue to pose a threat to the stability of the region until Kony is brought to justice and the LRA is diminished to the point it is unable to be reconstituted.

With U.S. support, the African Union Regional Task Force (AU-RTF) has significantly degraded the LRA's capacity to launch attacks on civilians and we have witnessed a sharp increase in LRA member defections and captive releases. Over 270 people have either defected, escaped, or been released since 2012. The number of people killed by the LRA has dropped by 90 percent since 2010 (365 in 2010, 36 in 2014, and 19 through June 30, 2015). During this time, AU-led forces have removed four of the LRA's top five commanders from the battlefield, including the International Criminal Court (ICC) indictee Dominic Ongwen who defected in January 2015. In June 2015, seven members of Kony's personal security detail also defected. We estimate the LRA now has less than 150 fighters (plus another 150-200 women and children captives), compared to perhaps as many as 1,000 fighters in 2009. As of June 30, 2015, the United Nations Office for the Coordination of Humanitarian Affairs (UN OCHA) estimated that about 199,000 people were displaced or living as refugees across CAR, DRC, and South Sudan as a result of the LRA threat, a significant decrease from the approximately 326,000 displaced people reported at year-end 2013. These statistics make it clear that our approach is working, but Joseph Kony is still commanding the LRA and until he is brought to justice we remain committed to finishing the work we started.

Our many successes have changed the nature of the LRA threat to the region. Joseph Kony has broken the command structure into several small groups, spread across eastern CAR, DRC, and the disputed area of Kafia Kingi between Sudan and South Sudan. While these groups are still a threat to small communities, their attacks tend to focus more on supporting their own survival, rather than on spreading terror or attempting to grow back into the force they once were. These small groups are pressured by AU-RTF forces to keep on the move and have less and less contact with each other. While this hinders their ability to coordinate attacks, it also makes them more difficult to track and target, especially considering the size and inaccessibility of the LRA-affected region (approximately the size of California over extremely difficult terrain to transverse).

In a May 2015 UN Report, the Secretary-General, while emphasizing the successes of the counter-LRA effort, noted that the LRA continues to pose a regional security threat, particularly in CAR and DRC, by exploiting the lack of state authority and security gaps in remote parts of Central Africa, pursuing opportunistic alliances with other armed groups, and engaging in illicit trade. The LRA's presence in CAR ensured links with other LRA elements in DRC and facilitated trafficking of ivory, gold, and diamonds, including via the disputed Kafia Kingi territory between southern Darfur in Sudan and Western Bahr-al-Ghazal in South Sudan where the presence of senior LRA leaders continues to be reported.

The Department of State and USAID are supporting programs to promote the protection of civilians, along with the rehabilitation and reintegration needs of vulnerable communities in CAR, DRC, and Uganda. State and USAID are funding communication networks, including high-frequency radios, to enhance community-based protection in CAR and DRC. USAID is funding activities through the Secure, Empowered, Connected Communities Programs (SECC) in CAR and DRC and through the Supporting Access to Justice, Fostering Equity and Peace (SAFE) program in northern Uganda. The programs are moving ahead with community-based protection, reintegration, and social cohesion activities. USAID and State also continue to provide humanitarian assistance to internally displaced persons, refugees, host community members, and other populations affected by the LRA.

The United States can and will continue to provide critical capabilities and support to help them succeed in their efforts. Although we've witnessed many successes, we must not let up pressure and we must stay the course by getting Kony and helping to provide stability to the region in a post–Kony environment. This is the right thing to do.

Representative Smith, Ranking Member Bass, and Members of the subcommittee, thank you again for holding this hearing and giving us the opportunity to discuss our extensive engagement in the region. I hope this information is helpful to the subcommittee. I am glad to answer any questions you might have.

Mr. SMITH. Madam Ambassador, thank you very, very much.

I would like to now yield the floor to Special Envoy Perriello.

STATEMENT OF THE HONORABLE THOMAS PERRIELLO, SPECIAL ENVOY FOR THE GREAT LAKES REGION OF AFRICA, U.S. DEPARTMENT OF STATE

Mr. PERRIELLO. Chairman Smith, and members of the subcommittee, thank you so much for the invitation to testify today and for your unwavering interest in the comprehensive efforts to support peace, democracy, and development in the Great Lakes region. I am honored to be back on Capitol Hill to have this opportunity to serve and to get to testify here today with one of the true all-stars of the foreign service, Assistant Secretary Linda Thomas-Greenfield.

As she outlined, we greatly appreciate the broad support from Capitol Hill for our engagement, our values, our programs and our Embassies in the region. After decades of instability, and of international investment in peace, the next 2 years will determine much about the future of the Great Lakes region. The run-up to elections in the Republic of Congo, the DRC, Rwanda, and Uganda, and the ensuing crisis from Burundi's discredited elections, will determine much about whether the region will reap the benefits of decades of investments in security and democracy or rather trade in that hard-fought progress for the entrenchment of individual leaders. It is for this reason that I am focusing my testimony today on these upcoming elections and our efforts to support them, although I will be more than happy to answer questions on other issues afterwards.

The crisis in Burundi is a prime example of what happens when an individual clings to power at the expense of his country. President Nkurunziza's decision to stand for a third term and violate the Arusha agreement has triggered a complex and dire crisis. Months of government repression, a failed coup attempt, discredited elections, tit-for-tat assassinations, and a mounting humanitarian crisis leave Burundi facing a shorter and shorter fuse.

Open political space has been all but eliminated in Burundi, creating an environment of intimidation and fear where daily violence and assassinations have become the norm. Much of the violence is reportedly carried out at the hands of state security services in the Imbonerakure, the armed wing of the ruling party's youth militia, but also by groups aligned with different political parties acting in retaliation. Their actions risk an expanded civil war as well as state failure.

While Burundi's past conflicts have been marked by horrific ethnic massacres, the current crisis has thus far avoided this element. However, we worry with continued instability the risk for the conflict to take on an ethnic component grows. Perhaps most pressing, Burundi's economy is in free fall which will continue to exacerbate the suffering of the Burundian people, already among the world's poorest, many of whom suffered from malnutrition even before the crisis.

We generally support regional leadership in resolving conflicts. However, certain regional dynamics in this case are impeding progress. Those in the region interested in testing their own country's term limit provisions are watching Burundi out of their own self-interest. Those supporting Nkurunziza also argue that our focus on term limits comes at the expense of stability. But the facts prove quite the opposite. Regular, democratic transitions of power are in the best interests of a country's stability. No credible observer thinks Burundi would not be better off if Nkurunziza had allowed constitutional elections to proceed. The international community would be talking about targeted investments, not targeted sanctions. We would be talking about Burundi as a model, not as a cautionary tale.

There are also broader geopolitical dynamics in play here. Some countries side with Burundi's Government because they believe the instability is being driven not by legitimate discontent by Burundians, but by Rwanda's support for the opposition. This is reviving historic geopolitical fault lines and risks holding back regional consensus on next steps to resolve the crisis. We encourage Rwanda, Tanzania, and all neighboring countries to be a force for peaceful resolution.

We believe that an inclusive, immediate, and internationally-mediated dialogue amongst Burundian stakeholders under EAC and AU leadership is the best route to resolve this crisis. We were heartened to see strong leadership and consensus at the African Union last weekend when the Peace and Security Council called for the resumption of an inclusive dialogue to be held outside of the country under the facilitation of President Museveni. We support the AU's leadership in demanding more urgent progress toward dialogue and consequences for those who impede it.

Regarding our next steps, we are pursuing all available diplomatic tools to convince Burundian stakeholders, the region, and the international community to support the immediate resumption of dialogue. We have already significantly curtailed our security assistance to the Burundian Government and all remaining non-life-saving U.S. assistance is being reviewed. While we strongly support the peacekeeping missions in Somalia and the Central African Republic, our ongoing support for Burundi's participation could be suspended if the government continues on its current path.

We are reviewing options for holding individuals accountable for acts of violence and human rights abuses. In this effort, we support the AU's call for sanctions and the EU's recent decision to impose targeted sanctions to hold accountable those whose actions they determined have led to acts of unlawful violence and serious human rights abuses.

Lastly, the interagency is working with the White House on contingency planning for the possibility of more widespread violence in Burundi. We laud the AU for also pursuing such planning and we will support efforts to prevent mass atrocities.

Whereas Burundi has already made a costly decision to pursue a dangerous path, the leadership of the DRC still faces a choice, a crossroads, with its Presidential elections currently scheduled for November 2016. Good elections would bolster the DRC's democratic development and be a critical step in addressing governance issues that have been a fundamental aspect of decades of instability. On the other hand, a delayed or illegitimate election could set off a far greater crisis than we have seen in Burundi. The DRC Constitution states unambiguously that a President may serve only two consecutive terms in office and this provision cannot be amended.

The government's attempts to change the electoral process in a way that could extend President Kabila's tenure have been staunchly rejected by the population, many of the President's own political supporters, their Parliament, and civil society. There are technical challenges that must be addressed if national elections are to be held on time. The current bloated electoral calendar is already off track. The voting rolls have not been updated since the last elections and the Independent National Electoral Commission or CENI recently became leaderless with the resignation of its President, Abbe Malu Malu.

Beyond the timing and logistics of elections, the most concerning trend in the DRC is the alarming escalation of political repression and the closing of political space. Disturbing reports of extrajudicial killings, use of excessive force against demonstrators, and trumped up convictions of civil society leaders are all of serious concern.

The challenges outlined above are not insurmountable, but a 2016 election will require Congolese political leaders to quickly reach consensus on next steps. First, the DRC needs to revise a realistic electoral calendar which prioritizes Presidential and parliamentary elections next year and consolidates multiple rounds of voting.

Second, the DRC Government and the CENI should agree upon a budget and the government should disburse the necessary funds. Third, the CENI should green light a process for updating existing voter rolls. Fourth, candidates, parties, and government officials should all make a pledge for nonviolence. Fifth, the DRC Government should resume cooperation with MONUSCO to ensure proper security, given the acute risk of instability and violence during the election period.

We will continue to engage the DRC Government, CENI, opposition parties, and civil society to support the upcoming elections and to maintain and reopen political space. We will also continue to work with our donor partners on public engagement and electoral support. Our goal is simple: Let the voice of the Congolese people shape their country's bright future.

Finally, Rwanda's elections are not until 2017, but the Rwandan Government is already taking steps to enable President Kagame to remain in office beyond current constitutional term limits. While we respect the ability of any Parliament to pass legislation that reflects the will of the people, we continue to firmly support the principle of democratic transition of power in all countries and respect for existing constitutional term limit provisions. We do not support incumbents amending constitutions to stay in power as doing so undermines democratic institutions and is an ingredient for instability.

The fate of democracy in Rwanda is about more than just the next election. Political freedoms continue to be limited, creating an environment where open debate and disagreements about security and political issues are rarely seen. Respect for human rights is a pillar of democracy and credible elections.

Let me conclude these introductory remarks with a few general takeaways. First, countries in the region are watching closely what happens in Burundi and the Republic of Congo with their own elections in mind. Second, there must be consequences when leaders deliberately exchange their country's stability for their own hold on power. Sanctions and cuts to assistance as targeted as possible must be part of this equation. Third, courageous citizens across the region take great personal risk each day to defend fundamental freedoms and a future many of us take for granted, the Pierre Clavers, the Yves, the Freds. The future of the region will be forged by those who stand for a democratic future, but our policy can reinforce and protect their efforts. Fourth, high-level U.S. and international engagement will be pivotal between now and 2017 as the region is watching how donors respond to actions in the region.

Despite the worrying signs across the region, I want to end on a positive note. There is still a window for all Burundian stakeholders to come together in a dialogue before this escalates to war. There is time for the DRC to organize credible and historic elections to see the first peaceful democratic transition and for Rwanda's story to be one of great economic growth and democratization. But time is of the essence, as is strong bipartisan U.S. leadership. Thank you very much.

[The prepared statement of Mr. Perriello follows:]

Testimony
"Africa's Great Lakes Region: A Security, Political, and Humanitarian Challenge"
Special Envoy Thomas Perriello
U.S. Department of State
House Foreign Affairs Committee
Thursday, October 22, 2015

Chairman Smith, Ranking Member Bass, and members of the Committee: Thank you for the invitation to testify today on the many challenges facing the African Great Lakes region, and our comprehensive efforts to support a durable peace, strong democratic institutions, and shared prosperity, including through upcoming elections across the region. I am honored both to be back on Capitol Hill and to be asked to testify today with Assistant Secretary Thomas-Greenfield.

As the Assistant Secretary has outlined, the Great Lakes region has experienced a generation of tumult, but over the last couple of decades it has benefited from bipartisan support on Capitol Hill that has not gone unnoticed by the people of the region. Even in today's political climate, we see and greatly appreciate the broad support for our engagement, our programs, and our embassies in the region.

After decades of instability with devastating human consequences, the next two years will determine much about the Great Lakes region's future. Whereas in past years the story of the Great Lakes was one of active conflict, we have seen significant gains towards peace and stability in the region. While we continue to address armed groups, particularly in eastern Democratic Republic of the Congo (DRC), our attention is focused acutely at this time on related, underlying challenges: the establishment of strong institutions of governance and harnessing the power of democratic voices in order to ensure that the people of the region are empowered to determine their countries' futures.

In this regard, we are putting intense diplomatic efforts behind support for upcoming elections in the Republic of Congo, the DRC, Rwanda, and Uganda, as well as addressing the violent, destabilizing aftermath of Burundi's recent decision to proceed with what the African Union called "non-consensual, non-inclusive elections." The run-up to these elections – particularly with respect to leaders' decisions to respect constitutional term limits and governments' decisions to protect open democratic space, even for peaceful dissent – will determine much about whether the region reaps the benefits of two decades of investment in peace, democracy, and development, or trades in those hard-fought gains for the consolidation of power. It is for this reason that I will devote my testimony today to these upcoming elections, our efforts to support them and the efforts of more than 125 million citizens resident in the region who are demanding a voice in shaping brighter futures for their countries.

We know what could happen in the Great Lakes if these next elections are perceived as unfair, if leaders do everything they can to cling to power, and if citizens' voices are silenced. Sadly, the current crisis in Burundi demonstrates with stark clarity the human costs if leaders in the region attempt to change the rules to stay in power. The bleak situation President Nkurunziza faces should serve as a cautionary tale, not a playbook, for other leaders in the region. If the same situation unfolds in the DRC over the next year, the costs in terms of human life, economic well-being, and regional stability would be far greater. It is first and foremost the responsibility of these governments and their citizens to do the right thing – for presidents to respect constitutional term limits, for security forces to respect the rule of law and democratic freedoms, and for citizens to exercise their rights peacefully. But it is also our responsibility to support them and to help ensure that this pivotal period in Great Lakes history becomes the prelude to a new chapter of peace and shared prosperity, rather than a violent sequel of past instability and setbacks. The people in the region – with bipartisan support from the United States – have invested too much not to see the Great lakes through this promising though daunting period of transition.

Burundi

Political and Security Crisis

The political and security crisis in Burundi is a prime example of what happens when an individual clings to power at the expense of his country and people. President Pierre Nkurunziza's decision to stand for a third term and violate the Arusha Agreement, which led to the end of Burundi's deadly civil war and provided the foundation for a decade of progress, served as the precursor to this now complex and dire crisis. This focus of blame was recently confirmed in the African Union Peace and Security Council's October 17 communique. Months of government suppression of protestors, a failed coup attempt in May, which we strongly condemned, discredited elections held over the summer, tit-for-tat assassinations, and an increasingly dire humanitarian situation have turned Burundi into a pressure cooker that could burst any day.

Open political space has been all but eliminated in Burundi. The government's deliberate efforts over the past year to silence dissent through harsh crackdowns on political protests, closing of independent media, and intimidation of the judiciary and civil society have resulted in an environment where few feel free to speak up and those who do are often forced to flee the country. A member of Burundi's Constitutional Court fled the country in May after coming under enormous pressure and even death threats to rubber-stamp Nkurunziza's disputed candidacy. The country's former Second Vice President similarly fled the country in June after receiving death threats in the wake of his public opposition to Nkurunziza's third term. The climate of fear in Burundi has only become worse since the elections. Media outlets forced by the government to close in the run-up to elections have yet to reopen, and most independent journalists have fled the country under threat. Nkurunziza's has made clear that any individual who speaks out against the government or opposes the government's actions will be considered an enemy of the state.

The Burundian people are paying the heaviest toll for the government's overreach. More than 200,000 people have already fled Burundi, with more leaving every day. In my recent travels to the region, I met with Burundian refugees in Rwanda and in Tanzania. I heard harrowing stories of Burundians who were attacked by youth militia, women who were raped, and of families left behind. The refugees showing up in camps now are weaker, more malnourished and traumatized, and their willingness to risk everything to flee proves how harrowing the situation has become inside Burundi.

For those who do stay in Burundi, daily violence and assassinations have become the norm. We receive reports of dead bodies found in and outside the capital on a daily basis, many under conditions suggesting the individuals were targeted for political retribution. The assassination of General Adolphe Nshimirimana, the brutal assassination attempt on human rights activist Pierre Claver Mbonimpa and the fatal attack on his son-in-law, and the attempted assassination of Burundian military Chief of Staff General Prime Niyongabo are indicative of the ongoing violence. The next attack could unleash wider-spread violence.

Much of the daily, or more often nightly, violence is reportedly carried out by state security services, as well as at the hands of the *Imbonerakure*, the armed wing of the ruling party's youth militia. Reports of harassment, torture, and killings by the *Imbonerakure* go back months, with recent reports suggesting that the youth militia is being more widely used by the government to carry out targeted attacks. Despite repeated calls by the international community, neither the senior government leaders who control and orchestrate *Imbonerakure* violence nor members of the *Imbonerakure* themselves have been held accountable for any of the attacks allegedly carried out by this group. However, we also have credible reports that attacks have been carried out against Burundian security services, including police officers, by groups reportedly aligned with different political parties or in retaliation for attacks by police. The instability caused by this cycle of attacks, and widespread reports of groups arming in the countryside, demonstrates the real risk of devolution to a low-level civil war or effectively a failed state with pockets of ungoverned space. Reports that refugees are being recruited and armed by regional actors only compound the problem. Any effort to undermine Burundi's stability and democracy is condemnable and must stop immediately.

Perhaps the most pressing issue in Burundi right now is the dire economic situation. Put simply, Burundi's economy is in free fall. The Burundian government is struggling to pay salaries and its bills. Recent developments have crippled an already fragile economy, causing prices to spike in a country where the majority of the population lives on less than a dollar a day. A tipping point for the country could be when the government runs out of cash on hand, which may be only a couple months away.

Regional Dynamics

The crisis in Burundi, like any in the Great Lakes region, proceeds not in a vacuum, but within the context of important broader regional dynamics. As a general rule, the United States strongly supports regional leadership in resolving political and security crises. The region has the expertise, leadership, influence, and motivation to be the most effective in resolving a crisis within its own neighborhood. With Burundi, we note the engagement of the East African Community (EAC), the International Conference on the Great Lakes Region (ICGLR), the African Union (AU), and even the United Nations (UN). While we continue to work with and support our regional partners, we are concerned that some regional dynamics may be impeding progress in this case.

Many in the region who, like Nkurunziza, are testing the fortitude of their country's term limit provisions, are watching Burundi in hopes that it helps set a precedent for individuals remaining in power. The governments of the Republic of Congo and Rwanda are already making moves to amend their constitutions, while senior political figures in the DRC have indicated an interest in doing so.

Others in the region, often those supporting the Burundian government, argue that our focus on term limits comes at the expense of stability. We argue quite the opposite – support for regular, democratic transitions of power is in the best interest of a country's stability. Burundi is a prime example of the instability that comes when a president tries to stay in power at the expense of his country. It is naïve to believe that violating term limits in other countries will be met with drastically different results than it has in Burundi.

These same dynamics are exacerbated by the arguments from some in the region that the Arusha Agreement should not be considered sacrosanct. The Arusha Agreement contains no ambiguity about limiting presidential mandates, so it is not a complete surprise that those backing Nkurunziza are downplaying the immutability of Arusha. Given Arusha's critical role in ending the civil war, its strong influence of the subsequent constitution, and its continued prominence in Burundi over the past decade, we believe its preservation is paramount as stakeholders work to resolve this crisis.

There are also broader geo-political dynamics at play in Burundi. There are reports that Burundian opposition figures are residing in Rwanda and receiving support from the government there. This is increasing regional tension as countries side with Burundi because of their opposition to perceived Rwandan involvement. This type of tension is not new to the region; indeed, historic geo-political fault lines that go back at least to the Congo wars risk being revived today. There are increased indications that the EAC is divided along these predictable fault lines, preventing a consensus on moving forward. It is imperative that the EAC, in coordination with the AU and the UN, reach consensus and urgently move forward to resolve this crisis, and restore stability and cooperation to the region. In this regard, we were heartened to see strong leadership by the AU just last weekend, when the Peace and Security Council in a strongly-worded communique called for targeted sanctions against Burundian actors undermining the search for peace, an increase in military and human rights observers in Burundi, robust contingency planning for increased violence, and most urgently, the resumption of an inclusive dialogue amongst all Burundian stakeholders to be held outside of the country.

Need for Dialogue

Indeed, we believe that this type of inclusive, immediate, and internationally-mediated dialogue among Burundian stakeholders is the best route to a consensus path forward for the country and regional stability. To ensure that all peaceful parties participate and feel safe, we support the dialogue being convened outside of Burundi and with an African mediator. The EAC has long agreed on the need for dialogue, having appointed Ugandan President Museveni back in July to facilitate it. President Museveni has since repeatedly affirmed his intention to convene the dialogue, and the AU last weekend put its support behind Museveni's continued leadership. While we support President Museveni, and his regional mandate as facilitator, we have been frustrated by the failure of such talks to begin and believe the people of Burundi cannot afford further delays in resolving this crisis.

The Burundian government and opposition parties rejected two previous UN envoys sent to Burundi to help mediate dialogue prior to this summer's elections. This dynamic, coupled with the prospect that any dialogue may fail in the end to achieve peace, may be contributing to the delay in the launch of the dialogue. If President Museveni and the EAC prefer, we would support the AU assuming facilitation, in order to jump-start the process. Also, while we support the dialogue being convened in Uganda, we would similarly support the region accepting the AU's offer for the dialogue to be convened in Addis Ababa at their headquarters. The scarce resource here is time. We fear the window is closing for restarting a dialogue in time to prevent wider-spread violence.

Once a dialogue is initiated, we can work with the region to build the necessary infrastructure around it. The international team of envoys is available to support and observe the talks, and we have worked with regional bodies thus far to find a path forward. The right participants can be worked out through initial discussions, including the right leaders to represent the array of peaceful opposition parties. The issue of term limits will need to be addressed, but should not be the first or only item on the agenda. We do not want the most challenging factors to hold up the dialogue or prevent resolution of other topics, including reopening the media, releasing political prisoners, and disarming youth militias. Opposition leaders have told me they are prepared to begin talks immediately without pre-conditions. The Government of Burundi has told us that it supports an internal dialogue under its conditions, but, under increasing pressure from the recent AU communique, has recently indicated that it too is open to an international dialogue. Again, the imperative here is time. The onus is on the region to urgently convene the dialogue, and on the Nkurunziza regime and the Burundian opposition to come to the table in good faith.

Next Steps

Regarding our next steps, first and foremost, we are pursuing all available diplomatic tools to convince stakeholders in Burundi, the region, and the international community to resume immediate, inclusive, regionally-mediated talks to end this crisis. I just returned from the region where I met with members of the Burundian government, civil society, and opposition members. Our Ambassador and her team in Bujumbura are doing an outstanding job with limited personnel and under very difficult circumstances. We must maintain lines of communication with the government as we encourage them to do the right thing. We must also continue to engage civil society and the opposition to convince them that peaceful avenues to resolve this crisis remain imminent and viable.

Similarly, we will continue to engage with all the regional stakeholders, as we cannot resolve Burundi on our own, nor should we. The AU and the EAC must retain the lead in resolving this crisis, and we will continue to support their efforts to convene a dialogue, respond to the mounting humanitarian crisis, and undertake contingency planning.

We have already significantly curtailed our security assistance to the Burundian government, including International Law Enforcement Academy and Anti-Terrorism Assistance training that we provide to Burundian law enforcement agencies, in-country training for the Burundian military under the Department of Defense's Section 2282 Train and Equip program, which has helped prepare Burundian peacekeepers for missions in Somalia and the Central African Republic (CAR), and training and assistance under the Africa Military Education Program. Our remaining assistance is primarily going to International Military Education and Training activities, which help increase the Burundian military's understanding and acceptance of civilian control of the military, human rights, military justice, and management of defense resources. While we strongly support the peacekeeping missions in Somalia and CAR, our support for Burundi's participation could be cut if the government continues down its current path. All non-life saving assistance and the country's eligibility for African Growth and Opportunity Act benefits are on the table.

We support the EU's recent decision to impose sanctions and hold accountable those whose actions it has determined have led to acts of unlawful violence, repression, and serious human rights abuses in Burundi. We strongly support the AU's decision to pursue sanctions as well. We have repeatedly called for accountability in Burundi and will continue to support measures aimed at doing so. There should be consequences for those who blatantly destabilize a country. The EU has also begun Article 96 proceedings, which could lead to the suspension of the EU's remaining assistance.

Lastly, we continue to undertake contingency planning for the possibility of more widespread violence in Burundi and support additional efforts by the AU in this regard. The Atrocities Prevention Board (APB) has been actively seized with

Burundi for over a year now. The State Department, DOD, and USAID are working closely with the White House to ensure that we are prepared to respond to changing conditions on the ground. We will do everything we can to support the people of Burundi and prevent mass atrocities.

The DRC

The Stakes

If Burundi demonstrates the costs of a country choosing the wrong path, the DRC is at the crossroads, still within sight of the right course. DRC's presidential election is currently scheduled for November 2016, providing an opportunity for the first peaceful democratic transfer between elected leaders in the DRC's history. It is essential that the DRC government avoid the path taken by Burundi and use this next year to implement a plan for peaceful, credible, and on-time elections in line with the constitution.

The stakes are enormous. Good elections would bolster the DRC's fragile democratic progress, continued stabilization across the country, the confidence of investors, and momentum towards greater development and prosperity. Alternatively, a failed, delayed, or illegitimate election could set off violence and repression on a much larger scale than we have seen in Burundi. In a worst-case scenario, the size of the country, the sheer lack of infrastructure, particularly in remote provinces, the litany of arms available, the continued predations of armed groups, and the history of violent conflict could make DRC ripe for widespread instability and atrocities if the government resorts to repressive tactics to remain in power. Such instability would almost certainly reverse the security gains, economic growth, and political reform achieved in recent years. It could also have dangerous repercussions for the region, expanding already high refugee flows on overburdened neighbors and leaving cross-border armed groups unchecked.

We remain hopeful that President Kabila will do the right thing and ensure that his country undertakes national elections in November 2016 within constitutional parameters. He has made no declarative statement that he intends to do otherwise. However, the government has taken a number of troubling steps, which threaten a constitutional electoral calendar and are widely perceived as means to extend the President's hold on power.

The DRC constitution's term limit provision is unambiguous. A president may serve two, and only two, consecutive terms in office, and this provision cannot be amended without voiding the entire constitution. Any effort to overcome the term limit or delay elections certainly will be met with a strong reaction from the people of the DRC, as earlier efforts have demonstrated. I met many of them during recent trips to the Congo, and it was clear that there is massive, widespread support for a free and fair democratic transition and for protecting the constitution. Indeed, giving voice to the Congolese people to freely choose their leaders is the fundamental bedrock of our policy in the DRC.

An attempt by President Kabila's political supporters in 2014 to amend the constitution stalled due to disagreement within his political alliance. In January 2015, President Kabila's "Presidential Majority" coalition introduced electoral legislation requiring a nationwide census that would have significantly delayed elections past November 2016. Following widespread and violent protests around the country, the DRC Parliament removed the census language from the legislation that eventually passed. Earlier this year, President Kabila initiated a National Dialogue to address concerns about the viability of the current election plans, but failure to agree with any major opposition groups on the format and agenda has undermined efforts to create delays. Most recently, senior leaders in Parliament and the Congolese government have been dismissed or forced to resign following the publication of an open letter by a group of parties within the ruling coalition calling for constitutional term limits and timelines to be respected.

This dynamic political situation means that the current electoral calendar is already off track, and it includes multiple rounds that could be consolidated or scheduled for after the presidential election. While properly timed, credible local elections could go a long way in decentralizing power across the DRC and strengthening the country's governance, rushed local elections could have the opposite effect of locking in patronage networks and ethnic divisions. In my travels, I have found almost no support for rushing local elections, and broad support for prioritizing presidential, parliamentary, and provincial elections in one or no more than two cycles.

There are a number of technical challenges that also must be addressed to meet the constitutional calendar, most notably updating voting rolls to include the eight million voters who have come of age since 2011. This will also likely include cleaning up the existing voter files needed for any election to be credible.

The National Independent Electoral Commission (CENI) recently became leaderless with the resignation of its president, Abbé Malu-Malu. A fully staffed and funded CENI is paramount to organizing good elections. It is unclear who will replace the former President, but the independence and qualifications of the final candidate will be indicative of the government's seriousness in supporting on-time, credible elections.

Beyond the timing and logistics of elections, the most concerning trend by the DRC government has been the alarming escalation of political repression and intimidation, closing political space for the opposition, media, and political activists. Disturbing reports of extrajudicial killings and disappearances; curbs on freedom of speech, assembly and the press; use of excessive force against demonstrators; politically-motivated prosecutions and surveillance of activists and opposition leaders, are all of serious concern.

In view of this challenging electoral environment, it is all the more important to retain a robust and capable UN Organization Stabilization Mission in the DRC (MONUSCO). MONUSCO played a pivotal role in the 2006 and 2011 elections, providing technical support, air assets for moving ballots, and civilian security. MONUSCO's good offices, logistical support, monitoring capabilities, and technical capacity are all useful tools to help ensure a peaceful and credible electoral cycle.

Next Steps for the DRC Government

The challenges outlined above are not insurmountable for the Congolese. There remains time for the government to organize credible, on-time elections next year, but the time for moving forward is now. Quite simply, DRC elections must be a 2015 priority issue to have a chance of being a 2016 reality. A 2016 election will only be possible if Congolese political leaders reach consensus on a number of steps over the next few months.

First, the DRC needs a revised and *realistic* electoral calendar, which prioritizes presidential, parliamentary, and provincial elections. Second, the government of the DRC and CENI should agree on a plan for disbursement of resources in support of the election cycle, and the government should promptly disburse the necessary funds. Third, the CENI must greenlight a process for updating existing voter rolls with urgency. Fourth, candidates, parties, and government officials should all make a pledge for nonviolence, with a paramount burden on the state to protect open democratic space.

Fifth, the DRC government should resume cooperation with MONUSCO. While the DRC has made significant democratic strides in the past 15 years, it has never conducted elections without experiencing electoral-related violence. We will need a robust peacekeeping mission to help ensure stability and the protection of civilians during this period, and to provide good offices and logistical assistance to facilitate the electoral cycle. Cooperation between the mission and the government will be key to planning for and providing electoral security, and responding to outbreaks in violence.

U.S. Next Steps

For our part, we will continue to engage the DRC government, CENI, opposition parties, and civil society members to support the upcoming elections and to maintain and reopen political space. Our goal is simple – let the voice of the Congolese people shape the country's future. On my recent visits to the DRC, I have been greatly impressed by the expertise, activism, and commitment demonstrated by the Congolese civil society, citizenry, and opposition parties, as well as many government officials. Grassroots organization is strong in the DRC, as is public understanding of what is at stake for their country. We will continue to advocate for the opening of political space and for accountability for any who repress democratic voices or advocate violence.

We will also continue to work with our donor partners on public engagement and electoral support. Many donors are rightfully concerned about putting money towards these elections until the government shows more commitment to ensure a credible and on-time process. While we share these concerns, we believe immediate investment in updating of the voter rolls is a priority and has the largest potential for costly delays, if not initiated early. We are currently funding programs that support election observers, voter education, political party training, and technical support to the CENI, and have additional human rights and judicial programming in the pipeline. We will continue to look for such opportunities to help.

Given what is at stake with these next elections, we should not resist using every tool available to support this historic electoral cycle. The stage is set for President Kabila to make the right decision, for elections to be a success, and for the DRC to welcome in a new era of development and prosperity. But, Burundi serves as a warning of what can happen when a government chooses the wrong path.

Rwanda

Rwanda's elections are not until 2017, but the government is already taking steps that would allow President Kagame to remain in office beyond current constitutional term limits. President Kagame and the Rwandan Parliament established a Constitutional Reform Commission (CRC), and the Rwandan Supreme Court ruled on October 8 that the current constitution permits reform of the term limits provision, provided certain steps are taken in line with the constitution. Proposed amendments to the Constitution were sent to Parliament for debate and consideration by the CRC on October 12. Our position here remains the same as in other countries in the region. While we respect the ability of any parliament to pass legislation that reflects the will of the people, we continue to firmly support the principle of democratic transition of power in all countries through free, fair, and credible elections, held in accordance with constitutions, including existing term limit provisions. We do not support incumbents amending a constitution to extend their hold on power. We believe doing so undermines a country's democratic institutions and stability. As President Obama said during his speech to the AU earlier this year, "When a leader tries to change the rules in the middle of the game just to stay in office, it risks instability and strife – as we've seen in Burundi. And this is often just a first step down a perilous path."

While Rwanda is pursuing an amendment process consistent with its constitution, the result may well be the same over time. Time and time again we see leaders sacrifice a country's progress, credibility, international standing, and economic, social, and political development in order to remain in power. A country - and a president - proves its strength not by amending its constitution, however lawfully, nor by the leader clinging to power for decades, but by respecting the rule of law of their own constitution, and by reinforcing and strengthening the democratic institutions that will ensure a stable, secure, and durable future for their country and people. Only through building those strong institutions and systems, and trusting in them and the people of the country to carry them forward, will sustainable democracy, development, and security be achieved.

We will continue to let the Rwandan government know our concerns about its efforts to pave the way for President Kagame to remain in office after 2017. President Kagame himself has repeatedly stated his commitment to respecting constitutional term limits, and we expect him to follow-through on that commitment, regardless of whether the constitution is amended. President Kagame said, "I am President because circumstances propelled me into that, but it's not something I am dying for. I cannot be here and say I must be President for life."

The fate of democracy in Rwanda is about much more than just the next election. Political freedoms continue to be limited, creating an environment where open debate and disagreements about security and political issues are rarely seen. Respect for human rights is a pillar of any democracy and a key aspect in evaluating the credibility of any election. As we told the Burundian government and continue to tell the DRC government, an election is about more than the day ballots are cast, it is about the process and the ability of citizens to have their voices heard without harassment or fear of persecution. A democracy proves its strength when it fully respects and upholds the freedom of expression by empowering citizens and members of the press to report on and discuss issues of public concern, however critical of the government.

We will continue to engage the Rwandan government and ruling party about human rights and democratic principles. As with Burundi and the DRC, we will also engage with civil society and opposition members. Improved respect for human rights is one of our top priorities for Rwanda. Rwanda has a once in a century opportunity to solidify the progress it has made over the past two decades and ensure the cementing of the democratic institutions and systems of the country into a firm foundation for the future. It can do this through a peaceful transition of power.

Takeaways from the Region

These three case studies leave us with a number of observations. The first, and perhaps most important for purposes of U.S. policy, is that countries in the region are watching what happens in Burundi very closely and will similarly watch what happens in the Republic of Congo and the DRC. Countries are watching not only what steps other governments take, but what consequences are suffered from it. While Burundi is on the precipice, the fact that Nkurunziza has thus far managed to stay in power should provide no solace to others who are considering the same course of action. The Burundian crisis demonstrates that the consequences of this course include a collapsing economy, widespread insecurity, dire humanitarian consequences, targeted economic sanctions, and isolation from traditional partners.

This leads to the second observation, which is that there must be consequences when governments deliberately harm their own country to stay in power. A single individual should not be able to send 200,000 of his citizens fleeing the country, create conditions in which hundreds of lives are lost, and suffer no consequence. The EU's decision to impose sanctions, perhaps followed by the AU's, and donors' decisions to suspend assistance are important in this regard.

The third observation is that high-level U.S. engagement will be pivotal between now and 2017. The region is keeping an eye on how we respond to actions in the region. President Obama's remarks at the AU were widely circulated within the region and lauded by people, though not always by leaders, across Africa. This policy is well grounded in experience, constitutions, and local support, and we believe U.S. leadership has a crucial role to play during this historic period.

The fourth observation is that we must continue to work closely with the AU and donor partners to maximize our diplomatic leverage and ensure clarity of message. The active coordination and engagement by the international team of envoys and the International Great Lakes Contact Group are pivotal here. I have been impressed by the level of daily coordination amongst these groups and believe our own engagement advances and is advanced by it.

The fifth observation is a well-known one, and that is that courageous citizens across the Great Lakes region take great personal risk each day to defend fundamental freedoms and a chance for a peaceful, prosperous, and democratic future. Heroes like Pierre Claver Mbonimpa and countless others face great personal risk to defend freedoms and a future that so many of us take for granted. The future of the region is forged by these leaders, but our policy can reinforce and protect their efforts.

Despite the worrying signs across the region, there remains time for each country to forge a positive path forward. Even in Burundi, there is a narrow window to opt for inclusive, immediate, and regionally-mediated dialogue to chart a consensus, peaceful path forward for the country. The DRC can still organize on-time, credible, and historic elections that put it on the path to realizing its bright and prosperous potential. And Rwanda's story could still be one of great economic growth *and* democratization, if the government prepares now for a 2017 transfer in executive power and commits to the protection of human rights and civil liberties. But time is of the essence, as is strong U.S. leadership and continued bipartisan support for our partnership with the people of the Great Lakes region.

Mr. SMITH. Without objection your full statement will be made a part of the record as well as yours, Madam Ambassador.

Let me just ask a few opening questions. First of all, we did have a hearing on the LRA on September 30 and there was a consensus among our witnesses that not only elimination, but even a limitation on the current U.S. deployment could be catastrophic. And I just hope you can reassure us that that is not in the offing. And you point out and the evidence is very clear, there has been a 90 percent decrease in killings, a 30 percent decrease in attacks by the LRA since deployment in 2011. And yet, there has been, not an increase, but a troubling number of abductions, particularly of Congolese that have occurred over the last 4 years, 417 was the number that was cited to us.

And I am just wondering, one of the things that came out of that hearing as well was the importance of U.S. leadership, the Ugandans, and the others who have very capable troops deployed as to how it really—that could all fall apart, too, without the U.S. command and control and some of the other counterinsurgency expertise that is brought to bear. So if you could just speak to that and how important that deployment has been and hopefully will continue. How well the other nations have stood-up troops because again, we don't want those troops to go away, we want them to stay focused until Kony is brought to justice as well as those who have committed atrocities.

Ambassador THOMAS-GREENFIELD. Let me just say that we are very proud of what we have achieved so far. Again, we don't want to sit on our hands and pat ourselves on the back yet because Kony is still out there. And as long as Kony is still out there, we remain committed to working with governments in the region to address this issue. We believe that our comprehensive strategy incorporating military and civilian efforts are helping the regional governments make significant progress to degrade the LRA's capabilities and reduce the threat that they pose to the communities around them.

And I want to note that we conduct regular interagency reviews to ensure that this effort is making sufficient progress. Our most recent review concluded that it continues to do so. So we will continue to remain committed to this effort. I have had several meetings with President Museveni over the past few months and raised this issue with him and got his commitment that he was willing to stay the course until Kony was captured. And so I think we are in a good place.

Mr. SMITH. On the issue of adoption, we held a hearing on July 16th with a focus on African adoptions in general and the DRC in particular. And the concern expressed by parents and families who actually know their children, but can't get that permit to allow them to leave the country. Peter Pham of the Atlantic Council who has appeared before our subcommittee many times, recently wrote an op-ed accusing Kabila of blocking the departure to the United States of legally-adopted children as a form of blackmail against pressure to follow the constitution.

If you could just provide further insight as to what is causing— the factors that are causing the ability of these children to find that loving home that just awaits them and whether or not Dr.

Pham is raising a legitimate point with regards to the reason, or one of the reasons, why Kabila is dragging his feet?

Ambassador THOMAS-GREENFIELD. I don't know that I could speak for the motives of President Kabila and the Government of the DRC, but I do want to say that we have put undue pressure on the government to relinquish these children and to allow them to exit the country. President Obama called President Kabila to urge him to action. Secretary Kerry has pressed Kabila to resolve this matter. We have had the Assistant Secretary for Consular Affairs travel to the DRC in March. In August, we had one of my deputies, Stu Symington, also engage with the government when he was there. Dr. Jill Biden sent a letter to President Kabila and to his sister to encourage him. Special Envoy Perriello has visited and he raised this issue.

And during the U.N. General Assembly last month in New York, both of us met with the government, with the Foreign Minister and we put this first on our agenda, which surprised him, that this was at the top of our agenda. We had a meeting for probably 1½ hours and the top subject, more than 30 minutes, was on adoption issues. What we are hearing from the government, and we continue to hear from the government is soon they are going to make a decision. Soon has not come soon enough for the families.

Mr. SMITH. Sure. What are the reasons? And I know some of the kids actually passed away from illnesses that could have been mitigated and probably eliminated.

Ambassador THOMAS-GREENFIELD. Part of the reason again, and I don't want to speak for the Government of the DRC, but they have argued that some of the adoptions were not done legally and because of that they want to investigate and ensure that legal procedures are used in the future. We are good with that, but most of these cases, in fact, probably the majority, if not all of our cases, were done in a legal manner and we are just asking that the government to release these children. They are still approving new cases which is a real problem for us because then it is causing more families to go through the anguish that they are going through. And many of those families are living in the DRC with their children, taking care of their children so that they can ensure their health and well-being.

Mr. SMITH. But the ongoing approvals would suggest that it is a delay, not a stoppage.

Ambassador THOMAS-GREENFIELD. That is my hope and prayer, but it is still taking way too long.

Mr. SMITH. Let me just ask you with regards to Burundi, on July 2, obviously, the administration and State Department announced the suspension of several security assistance programs. What conditions must be met by the Burundian Government in order for the U.S. Government to resume the security aid? And are there other sanctions potentially being contemplated now?

Ambassador THOMAS-GREENFIELD. Right now, what we are pushing the government to do is start a dialogue, an inclusive dialogue led by the Ugandan Government through the EAC. That would be the first step, but I think we have to wait and see what the results of that dialogue are before we get into any discussions with the government on next steps of resuming a normal relationship with this government.

Tom, you might want to follow up.

Mr. PERRIELLO. Sure. So a number of different programs have been suspended for a number of different reasons including security conditions on the ground, some of the multilateral lending institutions in the EU and others also have suspended based on everything from failure to meet the most basic transparency corruption standards, as well as obviously human rights and other concerns. The government, I think, would be mistaken to believe that they are within a step or two of such programs resuming, but the biggest step that could be taken as the Assistant Secretary mentioned would be the resumption of the dialogue and the moving toward again stability, as well as meeting that range of standards. And we are continuing to look at the full range of options that are available in terms of programs that are ongoing as well as looking at the leadership of the African Union and the European Union have taken, and holding people accountable, not just on the government side, but anyone also who is resorting to force or violence on the opposition side.

Mr. SMITH. Let me just ask you, when Rwandan Major Robert Higiro testified, we had vetted him very, very carefully and I know we asked the State Department to review his evidence which seemed very compelling. And my understanding is very clearly you found it to be credible. How has that affected our relationship with Rwanda? Have we raised it? What has the response been to these extrajudicial killings or the allegations of such? How do they respond to this?

Ambassador THOMAS-GREENFIELD. This is an ongoing subject with the Rwandan Government at every level. When we have had congressional delegations go out like Senator Coons who was out there a few weeks ago, in all of our engagements with the Rwandan Government, with the President, we have raised our concerns about human rights violations, about reports and allegations of extrajudicial killings, about disappearances. And they have denied their involvement in all of these cases. But we have been clear in our messaging that this will have a real deep impact on our future engagement with the Rwandans. They are doing some wonderful things on the economic and social front. They are making progress on the Millennium Development Goals (MDGs) like no other country. That is an amazing legacy that will be destroyed if on the political and human rights side they don't——

Mr. SMITH. I would suggest that legacy and I know Rick Warren has been very clear about this that it is only because—there is government commitment, no doubt. But it is the faith-based organizations that have made all the difference in the world. And I know, Tom, you might want to speak to that as well, that it has a multiplier effect. I mean Rick Warren recently brought a map and said here is where some of the government stations are for health and the like. Here is a map with stars or flags where there are faith-based communities that can take these challenges on and truly get it to the people. So I would encourage you to continue utilizing the faith-based community to the nth degree because I think the multiplier effect has no equal.

Mr. PERRIELLO. Sure, just to echo what the Assistant Secretary said, not just in Rwanda, but throughout the region we have emphasized several points, one of which is that fair elections don't just happen on election day. It is about the environment that is created in the months and the year ahead of an election. Is there open political space where dissent is welcomed, where assembly and press are welcomed? And we have seen in Rwanda, in DRC, in Burundi, obviously, past the breaking point that that political space is closing.

We have seen faith-based organizations play a tremendously positive role in all three of those countries including Rwanda and there has been an effort by leaders in multiple countries to say anyone critical of a government is immediately an opposition party member and this distinction between civil society organizations who are independent of political parties, but raising concerns about human rights, press freedoms, and other issues, as well in the Burundi case, of seeing anyone who is critical as being a putschist or a coup plotter. This is not what happens in stable democratic societies. All of us have faced more than a little dissent in criticism from political opponents and we have to understand that that is part of a healthy democracy. So we continue to raise that, not just for the Government of Rwanda, but governments throughout the region.

Mr. SMITH. I would say I am not sure we all welcome the opposition, but we certainly know that it is part of the system and it is an important part of it.

Mr. Cicilline.

Mr. CICILLINE. Thank you, Mr. Chairman. Thank you to our witnesses. Each of the countries that are the subject of this hearing face critical moments in terms of political transition. I just wonder if you would share with the committee what you think we might be able to do to encourage this democratic transition that seems to be up for consideration in each of these three countries and how we might use whatever tools are available to us to really encourage and persuade the leadership in these countries about the impact that that kind of peaceful transition has on the long-term security and prosperity of their country?

Ambassador THOMAS-GREENFIELD. I think the most important thing that we can do is to be consistent in our messaging. It has to come from every source within the U.S. Government. If we from the State Department are going out to meet with these governments, if members of other agencies are going out to meet with these governments, Members of Congress are going out, they have to hear to same message from all of us that we support democracy, we support stability, and we support countries honoring their constitutions and not changing their constitutions to benefit the incumbent who is in power. These countries are hearing these messages.

I like to refer to the fact that we have actually had some success. The one success we have had is that all of these countries have bought into the legitimacy of elections because in the past they didn't have elections. They would just declare themselves President for life and people would have to live with it. It is a small glimmer there, but the fact that elections provide legitimacy is an important thing and now we have to work to improve those elections, improve the ability of people in these countries to participate in elections and prove the ability of civil society to have a voice and then we will end up with examples like Nigeria. And I know we are not here to discuss Nigeria where civil society was a key player in that election, where capacity building was a key element in having a successful, democratic election that led to a peaceful transition.

Mr. PERRIELLO. Let me just offer a few things. One, I think to something Congressman Meadows said at the beginning. One of our biggest enemies here is apathy. And I think as we raise awareness, whether that is from the perch you have here or visiting the region, this is not something that has got the world's spotlight. There are so many crises around the world. The people of the region have struggled for a long time and forged a path forward and I think they deserve the world's attention. So I think that is one positive thing.

Second is while it is important for all of us as has been pointed out to call out backsliding in the region or closing of political space, there is also a lot positive to be said here. Everybody knows that this is a region with unbelievable potential, not just because of its mineral wealth, but because it does have strong leadership in civil society. It has really developed some of the institutions. Some are nascent of strong democracies. There are heroes who are risking their lives every day to defend basic freedoms and so I think we have a positive story to tell.

Third is continuing to be strong partners to the African Union as well as the European Union in these efforts. The African Union took quite bold leadership last week in its communique about Burundi and I think where they are willing to show leadership in the region across the continent, it is important for us to be there.

The last thing I just want to say is a shout out to supporting our Embassies there and particularly in Burundi that has been under difficult circumstances with security risks and drawdowns, a lot of long hours. When I go out and visit, they always welcome me even though I know it is exhausting for them to have visitors. And so continuing to be supportive of our folks that are out there under difficult circumstances.

Mr. CICILLINE. Thank you. And this spring, MONUSCO helped facilitate the release of 431 child soldiers from rebel groups in eastern Congo and the U.N. is currently working to help reintegrate these children back into society. Can you speak a little bit to how the United States is supporting efforts to disarm, demobilize, and reintegrate former combatants in the Congo, particularly as it pertains to children?

Ambassador THOMAS-GREENFIELD. That is one of our highest priorities in terms of working with governments on disarmament and demobilization. And USAID has a very robust program in DRC working in this area. I don't have the exact details. You were just out there. You may have more at hand. But it is something that we work very, very closely with MONUSCO on. We also are supporting UNICEF's efforts to help integrate these children back into their communities.

Mr. PERRIELLO. Yes, I just happened to be out at a project in Bukavu not long ago, just last week, it all bleeds together now, but it was an inspiring project, a local organization that had some support from both USAID and Eastern Congo Initiative that was working with both former child combatants, and also young women who had been in sexual slavery or otherwise put at risk. And it was skills training. And one of the things that people have learned over the years partly with support from our development organizations is it is not enough just to give the training. There has to be a demand side at the other end, an organization ready to hire them or some ability to allow them to start their own entrepreneurship operation. So this is incredibly important. It was something we certainly saw back when I was living in Sierra Leone as well, finding economic opportunities, but also community and support networks, psychosocial counseling, etcetera. So the United States, along with many other independent organizations, are doing great work on that, but I think it is also a reminder as we look at how crucial this democratic transition is that there continue to be elements that could become very problematic if the country started to backslide. And that is one of the reasons we have to stay so focused on the stability element as well.

Mr. CICILLINE. And finally, as you know, Uganda's Constitutional Court overturned their anti-homosexuality law. That was last year, but of course, we know that that doesn't end homophobic or anti-LGBT activities. So what is the current status of attempts to legalize homophobia and violence in Uganda? What do you think is the prospect that that issue will be raised again and is it a sentiment that is being reflected in other parts of the region that we should be aware of?

Ambassador THOMAS-GREENFIELD. We were very pleased when the Constitutional Court made the decision to not move forward with this bill and we have since heard from Ugandan authorities that they have no intention of presenting this bill back to their Parliament. That said, it always could happen again. We continue to support the LGBT community in Uganda, to encourage respect for their human rights. Human rights are enshrined in the Ugandan Constitution and so we constantly remind them that respect of the human rights of all Ugandans regardless of their sexual orientation or gender identity is critical to the country's success and moving forward in democracy. And I actually see this, at least up to this point, as a success story.

The LGBT community in Uganda have told us that they are seeing more support from the police. They feel much more confidence in the chief of police and they think his leadership has been part of building their confidence in the community. So we will continue to work this effort. It is not over. This doesn't change hearts and minds. There is still a huge, huge community of people who will express their views in ways that are unacceptable and what we want to do is encourage the government to hold them accountable, but also to protect the human rights of all of their citizens.

Mr. CICILLINE. Thank you. I yield back, Mr. Chairman. Thank you.

Mr. SMITH. Mr. Meadows.

Mr. MEADOWS. Thank you, Mr. Chairman. Thank you each of you for your testimony here today. I want to refocus on consistency of message and by addressing consistency of message, this is not

meant to be reflective of either of you because you have great re-
sumes and great credentials. But throughout administrations,
whether it is Democratic or Republican administrations, the consistency of message has not been something that the African communities, whether it is in these four countries or others, have been
able to count on. And it is very troubling to me as a Member of
Congress that when you go abroad, and specifically to Africa, the
continent of Africa and meet with leaders, the inconsistency of us
following through on what we promise is a reoccurring theme.

How can we address that to make sure that we are not saying
that we are making progress or making promises, only to find out
that part of our diplomatic and potentially political influence in
those regions are affected by our inability to keep our word?

Ambassador THOMAS-GREENFIELD. Thank you for that question.
I usually have someone walking behind me taking notes on promises that I make and they usually will nudge me.

Mr. MEADOWS. Can we borrow some of those?

Ambassador THOMAS-GREENFIELD. They will nudge me not to
make promises because if I make promises, we feel that we are
committed to following through on those promises.

What you are saying I hear regularly from African leaders. I
hear regularly that we have promised to support them in certain
areas and we have not followed up. On the other side of that coin
I hear from advocacy groups that we make promises to hold people
accountable and we don't always follow through in holding them
accountable and so that is on my shoulders to ensure that on both
sides.

Mr. MEADOWS. So if that is the case and I think that both of
those statements are probably accurate and there are times when
the countries do not do what they say they were going to do. How
do we just turn a blind eye to that and assume that we are going
to hit a reset button and then it somehow miraculously is going to
fix itself without identifying the issue and trying to address it? And
specifically, all we can do is control what we do. You have the per-
son that follows you around. So how do we do that that we let them
know that we mean what we say, that we are going to follow
through, whether it is accountability or funding or support in a
particular area?

Ambassador THOMAS-GREENFIELD. I am going to be honest and
frank. It is hard. And the reason it is hard is because we don't always have control over the resources and the resources are constantly a moving target. So there is a lot of manipulation of resources so that you can honor a commitment here which means you
might not be fulfilling the commitment here because you have
moved resources from here to honor the commitments that you
have made on this side of the ledger book. And that is part of not
having full control over the resources.

Mr. MEADOWS. You mean you specifically? Because it is a State
Department budget.

Ambassador THOMAS-GREENFIELD. The State Department specifically, but I would say me more broadly within my own small world,
not actually having control over those resources. So I say on a regular basis that my highest priority is democracy and governance to
really support governments building capacity and electoral commis-

sions and the capacity of civil society so that they can work to promote better democracy. But if you look at the pie chart, democracy and governance is the thinnest slice of the pie.

Mr. MEADOWS. Right.

Ambassador THOMAS-GREENFIELD. And so I will make commitments. There are elections all over the continent of Africa and everybody is asking for us to please send an observation team—send NDI, send IRI out to us, send the Carter Center out to us. And I am always nodding, I am going to do my best. And they take it as a commitment. And literally sometimes it is a matter of moving a commitment from somewhere else that may not be urgent at the moment and moving it over here to the urgent and then finding a way to deal with this when it becomes urgent. So that is part of the problem.

Mr. MEADOWS. Well, here is what I would offer and I will close with this offer and then one more question. As a Member of Congress, where we talk about apathy, it doesn't get me votes to be for foreign aid in Africa generally in North Carolina. I am willing to invest the political capital. I have invested the political capital. I am willing to work with the chairman and the ranking member because this is something that is near and dear to my heart and I am willing to do that.

If it means expanding some of those resources from other areas within the State Department where we can, as you put it, I think stay focused, I am willing to do that, but we need to know how we can best do that in a bipartisan manner. I am willing to ask the tough questions. I know that may come as a surprise, but I am willing to ask the tough questions to do that. But we have to do a better job of—and again, this is not directed at the two of you. We have to do a better job as a nation of saying what we are willing to do, following through on that so that they know that they can count on the word of the American people.

Now let me digress to one other area that you have already touched on and that has to do with the adoption of these children. Let me be perfectly clear for anybody that is here that is watching, this needs to go back. Enough is enough. We have to solve this problem. I am tired of coming to hearing after hearing after hearing and saying it is a high priority, it is our top priority, we are making progress where you got parents that don't believe we are making progress. And that message needs to be taken back. It will have financial ramifications and I am willing to stake my reputation on that. So if you will take that message back and I will yield back, Mr. Chairman.

Ambassador THOMAS-GREENFIELD. And I appreciate that message from you. When Tom and I were meeting with the Foreign Minister and we started on the subject and he said I can't believe you are going to start with this subject and I said I am going to be asked about this by our Congress. And I have to say that I started with this subject and got an answer from you. So your message has been heard.

Mr. MEADOWS. Well, tell him that we are going to look for answers, not that we are working on it. Delay is one of those things that everybody says we are working on it and the time is now for answers.

Ms. BASS. Well, Ambassador Perriello, your former colleague, Adam Schiff, sends his regards and actually is going to call you on that exact subject because he has constituents who have been trying to adopt from the DRC for quite a while. So I told him that I would relay that message to you.

Thank you both for coming and your time today. I might ask you a few questions that have already been asked since I came a little late, so forgive me if that is the case. But I wanted to first start by talking about Burundi and I know you gave an update on that, Madam Assistant Secretary, but I was just wondering what at this point do you think is our leverage in Burundi? And I know that the AU has certainly stepped up and I also know that we have suspended some assistance to Burundi, but do you think it is having an impact?

Ambassador THOMAS-GREENFIELD. Can I turn to my colleague to answer that?

Ms. BASS. Sure.

Ambassador THOMAS-GREENFIELD. He will give a better answer than I did.

Mr. PERRIELLO. I will try. First of all, please tell Congressman Schiff that I said hello. And I want you to know that I have a picture of one of the kids on my desk in the office.

Ms. BASS. That is good.

Mr. PERRIELLO. And I have met with the families and one of the first things Linda and I talked about is this is not technically in my docket, but they made clear this is an all team, all hands on deck effort. So all of us are participating in this. It boggles the mind that we are where we are and I have communicated to President Kabila directly that this is the number one thing I hear about from my former colleagues because that happens to be true as the message from Congressman Schiff indicates.

On the leverage with Burundi I think there are two——

Ms. BASS. I am sorry, before you go on to that, what do you think is the real hold up?

Mr. PERRIELLO. As Assistant Secretary Thomas-Greenfield said earlier, it is really difficult to know. While some people have posited that this is an effort to get a demand on this or that thing, it certainly has never been raised. We have gotten clear indications from people senior in the government that there is no legal barrier to this happening tomorrow, while others have certainly argued to us that there are these barriers. But as far as we can tell, there is nothing but political will that stands between at least some of the kids being released tomorrow, but I do want to let those who live and breathe this issue probably give more technical answers on it. But I can tell you that it boggles my mind.

Ms. BASS. You know, I went to one country, I won't mention the name of the country, not in Africa, and this issue was the same. And one of the things that was happening there was financial because a lot of the parents, people in waiting to adopt the children, were sending large sums of money to the country to maintain the children in orphanages. And it seemed as though there was a financial incentive from the people who ran the orphanages. I don't know enough about the situation in DRC to know if it is a similar thing that there are orphanages that people are running and U.S. citizens are supporting.

Ambassador THOMAS-GREENFIELD. There have been some allegations in that area and the fact that new adoptions are still continuing to be approved would suggest to us that that could be part of the problem because this is a business. And there are people who are benefitting financially from this and the more children they have in waiting, the more money they are getting. So I do see that as a real issue.

Ms. BASS. And the other side of it, too, is on our side and I am hoping that we are doing good jobs in screening who from here is adopting because we do have a problem on the other end, too, with some of the families here, then getting into trouble.

I wanted to—you were going to finish?

Mr. PERRIELLO. I was going to talk about the leverage issue with Burundi.

Ms. BASS. Yes, yes.

Mr. PERRIELLO. I think there are a couple of categories that we can think about. One is the various stakeholders in Burundi itself and the second is leverage we have with others who can be playing a positive or potentially negative role. And we talked earlier about how some of the actors in the region, that it is important to make sure that all the neighbors, whether that is Rwanda, Tanzania, Angola, DRC, are all being a force driving the stakeholders to a peace table. We believe that is best done in Kampala, although we would also support the African Union's call whether that is in Kampala or in Addis.

Within Burundi right now there are a number of drivers, one of which is economic collapse and while our direct aid has been suspended and the EU is going through its article 96 procedure, and obviously we try to coordinate and work not just with the AU, but donor countries. This is a government that is facing some real threats and challenges, not just physical security threats, but economic crisis.

We obviously continue to support the UNHCR efforts. I visited refugee camps in both Tanzania and Rwanda, camps with very tough conditions right now, not because the host governments aren't being generous, but because demands on UNHCR right now obviously with the Syria refugee crisis and other things are so high.

And so I think there is leverage that we have with various actors and one of the things we are trying to do is obviously maintain lines of communication and always provide a healthy outlet to a peaceful solution while making clear that there will be consequences for people both on the government and opposition side who try to escalate and we believe that some of those can be significant as well as support for other positive actors in the EAC and the African Union.

Ambassador THOMAS-GREENFIELD. If I can just add, I think the other leverage is to really put pressure on the region, on the EAC, on the AU that has been, I think, moving in a great direction, on the U.N. as well, to make sure that all of the players are actively involved in trying to find a solution and putting pressure on this government. They are feeling the economic pressure as Tom said.

They are feeling the economic pressure from the EU. They are feeling the economic pressure from the IFIs who have all pulled out their funding. And they are feeling the economic pressure from the private sector. So this is tremendous pressure, but it also shows the extent to which the President is willing to let the country collapse.

Ms. BASS. Wow. So in terms of what our direction is now, since they already had the election, the pressure and all and our leverage is about just making it peaceful, in other words? Because I realize that some of his opponents have mysteriously died and there have been ongoing attacks. Is that the direction?

Mr. PERRIELLO. The situation in Bujumbura is incredibly serious. In some neighborhoods we are almost to a position of ungoverned space where there is nightly violence and it is in both directions. There are people throwing grenades at police officers. Those police officers are going in and in some cases murdering entire families. In one case, that was someone with an IOM badge that had been shown to folks and the need for accountability that has been promised by the government.

The African Union put clearly the impetus for this crisis on the decision to go forward with what they called non-consensual, non-inclusive elections. We have reports from experts, as well as those looking at refugee flows, showing that the flow would probably be even higher if not for youth militias in the border areas, trying to prevent people from crossing so that the refugee crisis does not look as bad to the international community. So the situation is extremely serious. And in fact, to one of the things Assistant Secretary Thomas-Greenfield noted in terms of impact on the region, if I can be blunt, up until recently, there was a little bit of gamesmanship. It felt that people wanted to make this almost a proxy between scoring points with some of the neighbors and the closer this has gotten to widespread violence, some of those countries, I think, are switching to saying hey, let us not make this about each other, let us see this as a genuine crisis in Burundi that we cannot afford to see take on an ethnic or regional component. And so in that regard, you are seeing very serious issues.

However, we have not yet crossed the point of no return and we believe along with the African Union and others that the only thing that can prevent this from having an even more violent end is this inclusive immediate internationally mediated dialogue that the AU communique have called for.

Ms. BASS. Do you think that the goal of that would be new elections or the goal of that would be what?

Mr. PERRIELLO. So one of the things we have emphasized to President Museveni and others is that we don't need to solve those questions before the talks start, in part because getting people to the table is release valve to prevent folks from feeling force is the right way to solve this. However, we would be the first to admit those are going to be thorny and complicated questions. The opposition, at least through the CNARED coalition, there are complications of who should represent the opposition, initially said we want to guarantee that President Nkurunziza essentially immediately steps down and there is a transitional government. They have now said they would attend talks immediately without preconditions, but no doubt their position will involve some element of that, the government position will be quite different.

But the important thing is to get people at the table and see whether there is path forward that gets Burundi back on a path, that we have to remember for all the very scary situation we are in, 15 years of progress, 15 years of progress across ethnic divisions, a strong neutral military that is held together, some economic progress. Just a year ago, this is not the story we were telling about Burundi. And so that is what we hope is we can find that table that brings people back to that place.

Ms. BASS. Can you give an update on the situation in the DRC and Kabila?

Mr. PERRIELLO. So the situation in the DRC——

Ms. BASS. With regard to elections.

Mr. PERRIELLO. Right. Well, as I said if the Government of Burundi already chose to go down what we think was a very costly path, the DRC is still at that crossroads.

Ms. BASS. Right.

Mr. PERRIELLO. And it seems that there are some decisions to be made and certainly there are various moves that have been made by the government that would suggest heading in the direction of what is called glissement or slippage, but the reality is President Kabila has said over and over again I have never publicly said that I am going to break the constitution. I have never publicly said that I am going to run for a third term. We have seen most efforts at getting off a constitutional path have been successfully resisted by civil society and the opposition. It is a dynamic moment and I would say the next few months are going to be crucial. One of the mantras we have had is you know we need to think about DRC as a 2015 issue, not a 2016 issue.

The decisions, the hope of being able to see this historic democratic transition at the end of next year has got to be something that is in the next 2 or 3 months, getting this agreement from the electoral commission on the calendar, bringing people together, etcetera. So the situation, the stakes are quite high. They are far higher, obviously just by human count than in any other country in the region, but the good news is we are still in a place where a peaceful democratic transition could happen.

And I will just say, President Kabila, I think, deserves a lot of credit. Here is someone who as a very young head of his faction pushed for peace, got elected twice, has developed Kinshasa into a modern, very developed city. There is a lot to be said of building nascent democratic institutions, of going after at least some of the armed groups. And our hope is that part of that final legacy will be also to be the first to peacefully transfer power in DRC.

Ms. BASS. Well, then what is your assessment of the opponents? Is there organized, stable——

Mr. PERRIELLO. So a few things. One of the things that is very hopeful about DRC is that you see some of the core pillars of a strong democracy. You see a relatively free press. You see a civil society that is independent of all political parties. You see genuine opposition parties. You see a ruling coalition that is like a lot of unruly coalitions where even many of the key leaders in that party have broken from the President on some key votes. So when we think about it, it is not our job to figure out who the right candidate is. It is to let Congolese voices be heard.

What is concerning to us and we spoke about earlier is this issue about closing political space. There have been some dramatic steps taken, whether it is use of violence against protesters or surveilling and trumping up charges against civil society opponents. These are foundations of whether or not you will have a strong democracy.

President Kabila told me directly he understands that fair elections are about the space created in the year before an election and not just on election day. And we certainly will continue to work with the government on some of those factors.

Ambassador THOMAS-GREENFIELD. And I would just add that I am still hopeful about the DRC. We do have a window of opportunity and we have to continue to engage with President Kabila and the people around him to get them to do the right thing. They are at a fork in the road and they could take the right road or they can take the wrong road. But they still have a chance to take the right road and we have to keep pushing them in that direction.

Ms. BASS. Good. Well, finally, I just wanted to mention that and wanted to thank you, especially Assistant Secretary for allowing Anne Richard to come and to speak next week when we do one of our policy breakfasts because I am real concerned about the refugees. I mean there is an awful lot of attention on the Syrian refugees, very appropriately, but before there was the mass exodus from Syria, there was also a tremendous number of African refugees and I am just concerned that we might have lost sight of them. Lost sight of them in two ways. One, I don't know what is happening to them in Europe. But two, when we make commitments to increase the number of Syrian refugees, I think we also need to increase the number of refugees from the continent, especially those that are coming through Libya, but in general.

So a number of members signed a letter to Secretary Kerry asking for the numbers to be increased and I don't know if there is any update on that in that regard, if you wanted to comment.

Ambassador THOMAS-GREENFIELD. I will let Anne, who is going to come up and talk to you, give you the details, but I do know that the African numbers were increased in the coming year. I don't know where they are coming from, but they have increased them to 25,000 and I did carry a message from our earlier discussion back to the Bureau of Population Migration, and Refugees (PRM), so they are aware that you are interested in the subject and they are in a better position to discuss it with you. But I do think they heard your message.

Ms. BASS. Good. She will give us the latest update next Thursday. Thank you.

Ambassador THOMAS-GREENFIELD. And I will pass that back to her as well.

Ms. BASS. Okay.

Mr. PERRIELLO. Let me just add one thing on to that because when I was in the camps in Tanzania, they were some of the toughest conditions I have seen in an official UNHCR camp in a long time. And I think PRM and State deserve credit for pushing hard because all the attention had been on the situation in Europe. This was a question of trying to get an additional camp opened because I think there were 140,000 people in a camp that holds 30,000 at the time. And it was a matter of racing to get that open before the rainy season. And actually, in this case, the Tanzanian Government, particularly President Kikwete, deserves a lot of credit for pushing. There was a lot of regional resistance out in the west. So not just from the dollar figure numbers, but really trying to make sure there is attention in these spaces because the conditions are quite rough and the people coming over from Burundi now are coming over increasingly malnourished. Anecdotally, we are hearing increased incidents of gender-based violence. People are exiting because people are waiting to leave because of the fear of violence at the border. And therefore leaving sometimes in more vulnerable conditions.

Ms. BASS. And I appreciate that. I do just want to be clear that I was making reference to the ones crossing the ocean, coming into Europe. And I do think that many countries in Africa need to be acknowledged for the fact that they have been absorbing tens of thousands of refugees, but I remember a few months ago when 800 died crossing the Mediterranean.

Mr. SMITH. Thank you. Just a few final questions and of course, as my colleague says any additional questions. Thank you for your generosity for staying for long.

Let me just first of all, we did have Anne Richard testify. I chair the Commission on Security Cooperation in Europe and we had her testify on Tuesday on Syrian refugees and one of the biggest takeaways came from the UNHCR Representative Pitterman who said that the proximate cause for the mass exodus that has occurred is the 30 percent cut in the World Food Programme and that people are now to the point that if they don't have food, they are leaving. They just don't have food. Other necessities are scarce as well. And I am wondering what that cut has done to the four countries in the Great Lakes region, if you might want to speak to that. Because it seems to be catastrophic and they are doing it, obviously, the World Food Programme is trying to do a triage and figure out where do they put a dwindling number of monies.

And what also came across, and this was, again, from the UNHCR representative, is that they have only gotten 42 percent of their appeal for the Syrian refugees and the crisis in general, U.N., and that they are notoriously low on all of their appeals and that there are a lot of laggards who promise and never come through, but again, how does that affect the refugee situation and people who are at risk?

Let me also ask you with regards to the Scaling Up Nutrition program which we have had hearings on and we had several hearings on, as a matter of fact. I have introduced a bill called the Global Food Security Act which puts a heavy emphasis on the first 1,000 days of life, from conception to the second birthday, as being the all-important time to get it right for that child. Of course, you want to see nutrition and good supplementation for a lifetime, but that is where cognitive capabilities are either won or lost. That is where immune systems are built or not built and it mitigates, if not ends, stunting. And all four of the countries, Burundi in 2013, DRC in 2013, Rwanda in 2011, Uganda in 2011, all signed up for the Scaling Up Nutrition. And I wonder if you have any sense, does that come up in your meetings? Do we push it as a way? Because it not only makes sure that that unborn child or newborn child and that child as he or she matriculates into adulthood are healthier, but it has an unbelievably positive impact on maternal health and the woman and child or children, if it is twins, are that much healthier. Your sense on how that is going, particularly in war-ravaged Burundi where obviously these programs sometimes are short-circuited.

And finally, on the issue of trafficking, I am chairing a hearing on November 4 on trafficking, the TIP Report. I was the prime sponsor of the Trafficking Victims Protection Act, and frankly, found some flaws in this year's report which are not reflected in the narrative, but are reflected in the designations. I don't think any of the four countries that we are considering today were wrongly designated. Burundi is Tier 3. DRC is Tier 2 Watch List. Rwanda and Uganda are Tier 2.

But the Tier 3, I am wondering especially, Mr. Perriello, how often does that issue come up? Do you get support not only from the Embassy and the designated people at our Embassies that deal with TIP issues, but does the TIP office itself provide you with updates and guidance? And what has been the response from the governments in question? Because it seems to me sex and labor trafficking are among the most horrific human rights abuses on the face of the earth. Burundi is Tier 3 for both sex and labor designations and I just wonder if you might want to elaborate on how that plays into your efforts, both of your efforts in these countries?

Ambassador THOMAS-GREENFIELD. Let me start with the questions related to refugees and the impact of WFP's decreases. It is not in my portfolio, but it affects my portfolio. If affects the people of Africa. And it is across the board. It is not just in the four countries in the Great Lakes. We are seeing the impact in the refugee camps in Kenya. We are seeing the impact in the refugees camps in Ethiopia. And then worse, we are seeing a huge, huge impact on the Ethiopian population in terms of the possibility of a famine. So this is a very, very serious issue for us. It has a little bit to do with climate change, but it also has a lot to do with politics. It has a lot to do with political stability. It has a lot to do with government policies. And this is where I think we can make a difference in terms of getting governments to develop policies that target their communities and place agriculture on the top of their agenda in terms of building the capacity of people to produce their own food so that they are not dependent upon food aid.

I don't have anything on the malnutrition issue that you raise. If you don't mind, I would love to get back to you on that. That has not come up in any of my meetings with any of the governments. But I am sure my USAID colleagues hear it regularly.

Mr. SMITH. But again, if you could make it part of that. It seems to me that people sign up robustly with all kinds of good intentions which for whatever reason, different priorities, maybe apathy, and this program gets put on a shelf at least partially. And again, I don't know of a single program that I have ever seen that has done more and can do more to enhance the life, the well-being, and the mortality, the actual survival of individuals, children, babies, unborn babies, and then their mothers than this one.

Ambassador THOMAS-GREENFIELD. And I see this in terms of a political issue as well. And then on TIP, I had 50 meetings in New York during the ''speed meeting'' exercise that we went through and for every single country that was downgraded or not upgraded on TIP, I raised this as an issue. I will use the example of Comoros where there was an issue and they wanted to talk about how to address it and what they needed to do to address it so that they don't get downgraded even further. So we have found among African governments while they push back, they also take it very, very seriously because they know that we take it seriously.

So again, it is not always the best of situations, but I think governments are more and more taking it seriously. We hear a lot of arguments that this is our culture, you don't understand. It is not that we are trafficking in children. We are taking children from the village so that we can educate them, but you see no signs of the education.

So we do have this discussion on a regular basis with governments. And we work very closely with the TIP office to look at how we can help governments address this because our ultimate goal is to stop trafficking and to help governments address the issue and hold people accountable.

Mr. PERRIELLO. I would echo everything she said on TIP. I can't really be objective about it since I have been a big supporter of the program when I was on your side of things, but it certainly comes up with great frequency.

On your point of UNHCR and the 42 percent pledge, I will just note that at the time that I was in the camps in Tanzania they had only gotten 17 percent of their pledge for Burundian refugees. That has gone up a little bit with some help from the United States.

One thing I will just say in general with a number of things you are saying, and this takes me back a little bit to my previous job running Quadrennial Diplomacy and Development Review, is the attempt to use metrics in all of these situations. So whether it is WFP cuts or other things, I think we are trying to get better at some predictive analysis of being able to see when there is a drought in country X, how that is going to be affecting things 6 months, 12 months, 18 months out, and I think there is a lot that is useful in coming together.

One of the reasons we are still where we are in Burundi, I believe, is not just 15 years of investment on post-conflict transition, on reconciliation, on other things, but the Atrocity Prevention Board and other efforts flagged this a year out, 1½ years out, as meeting a bunch of indicators. It is where we are with DRC now. So I think all of this is part of that move.

And then last of all, I think to the point of some of the programs you are talking about, it might just be a moment to say we have spent 20 years as a country greatly invested in this region in terms of humanitarian support, as well as development, as well as security support. And as Linda mentioned earlier, underneath a lot of this is good governance. And we have done so much to get up to this point where there is a chance to turn the page where the dynamics are primarily determined by the region's future and not its past and some of that is the personalities involved and the dynamics. But underneath so many of these programs is a question of good governance.

Even with people who are desperately poor in Burundi, we cannot send that money to a government that is using it, funneling it in a different direction or not using it well or not being transparent. So that is why I think we come back to this idea that I think President Obama, with support from the Hill, has had a really good policy in focusing on constitutions mattering, rule of law mattering, term limits mattering. We are offering our advice to our countries in the region and we believe that his is an opportunity to make a real difference in those areas.

Mr. SMITH. One last thought before you leave, Ms. Bass, CRS's Sean Callahan testified on Tuesday and made a very important point that I have heard many times. You, I know I am sure, have heard it many times before, too. And that is the ability of faith-based groups, not only to be extraordinarily flexible and get more push, more outcome for the buck, but also the entre, the accessibility, the ability to do something in regions or places of conflict that perhaps other people wouldn't be able to do it because it happens to be a priest or a pastor of some kind or a bishop.

And I am wondering if you are finding in Burundi, for example, or any of these other countries, if the faith-based groups have placed a significant role and perhaps there is even a reason or cause for an enhanced role to make sure that the food, the medicines, whatever it might be gets from us and from other donors and the government and U.N., UNICEF, whatever it might be, to the intended recipient.

Ambassador THOMAS-GREENFIELD. I would say the faith-based NGOs, assistance groups, have been extraordinary and very, very supportive across the board in Africa. In the case of Burundi, you have a President who claims to be a believer. He preaches his beliefs and we need more voices in the faith-based community here in the United States to talk to him, to let him know that some of the things that he is doing are not acceptable and that it causes us to doubt his faith. People are dying, people are being killed and it is happening on his watch and he has a lot of friends here who are supportive of him and we would encourage that he gets some messages from that community to do the right thing for the people of Burundi.

Mr. SMITH. Mr. Clawson.

Mr. CLAWSON. No one likes the man or woman that comes in late and then talks a whole lot, right? Not great. Not good behavior. We always get multi-scheduled around here. You all know that already, right? So the fact that we come late or some folks, I don't know if Mark was here or not, that please don't take that as a personal reflection.

Mr. SMITH. As a former member, I am sure Tom understands that completely.

Mr. CLAWSON. You know the deal, right? And you know, you all are competing with Secretary Clinton, too, so you have tough competition today.

Mr. PERRIELLO. We were sure all those cameras were for this hearing.

Mr. CLAWSON. You are a smart guy. I wanted to make sure that I showed up for several reasons. Number one, I have a lot of respect for the chairman and the ranking member and you learn that this is a ''got you'' environment. If you ever say anything wrong, they got you, right? And I think this subcommittee has been one place where there is a little less of that. And they are trying to pay attention to an area of the world where in my view clearly we have not historically paid enough attention. So first thing is to show respect there.

Secondly, appreciation for what you all do to toil in and area or dedicated to an area that is not glamorous, but sure needs our attention as well. And to the extent that we can, resources which leads me to the third point and that is anything that I can do. This region of the world, your intersection of lots of humanitarian problems, ecological problems, and a big watershed all at the same place, right? And so we can't forget about it. And if I take too much more time after not being here for almost 1½ hours, I think it would be a little bit impolite. So with that, I express my appreciation to what you all are doing. And I say to the chair anything that I can do in this effort, of course, we stand ready. I yield back.

Mr. SMITH. Thank you, Mr. Clawson. Anything else you would like to say before we close?

Mr. PERRIELLO. I just want to add one quick note which was to your point about faith-based groups. I obviously agree, but the other group that I think can play a very constructive role in the region is the private sector. And in addition to looking at these democratic transitions, there is a tremendous amount of entrepreneurial activity for the small agricultural entrepreneur as well as for very large corporations. And one of the things we have heard a lot from the private sector is we need to get through these democratic transitions, get through that stability threshold to be able to really see the economic opportunity for folks. So that is another sector we are just engaging I wanted to mention.

Mr. CLAWSON. Could I jump in real quick? Spending my whole adult life in the private sector in the multi-national environment, we did business in South Africa, but nowhere else because we were worried about private property rights. And private business can always help in under-developed area because particularly if they have a little bit of enlightenment at the top so that all stakeholders mean something including employees, communities, etcetera. But you can never go to shareholders and say you may lose everything here because they don't respect, in this particular country or region, private property rights, right?

I know you are with me on this. Anything I can do in that regard, any help, if we can make the case for one of these countries that private property rights are respected, then the idea of exterior investment for the benefit of all stakeholders becomes lots easier to make.

For those of you in the audience that are from these countries, it scares private investors even for an export-based investment. It scares us to look at something like that because we are not sure that our private property rights, meaning our investment, and therefore our shareholders, would be protected if we set it up. I think there are plenty of investors that don't mind sharing with all stakeholders, including community and labor, folks that work. But you can't lose your investment. Does that make sense? So anything—we can take this offline, but any time I can help you all, I am on Chris' subcommittee here. Any time I can help in that regard, very, very interested in doing so.

Ambassador THOMAS-GREENFIELD. That is a strong message to give any time you have any contact with African leaders, they all want American investors. I hear it on a regular basis. I have participated in a meeting by the Initiative for Global Development's Frontier 100 Forum on business leadership in Africa that Secretary Albright and Colin Powell chaired yesterday. We talked about what would encourage American investors to go into Africa and what discourages them. And that point is the biggest point.

Mr. CLAWSON. This is the biggest point. And without this, the idea that Africa can self-develop in my mind is a long putt. And our intentions can be as wonderful as we want them to be. In our facility in South Africa, the government told us that we didn't have any choice but to sell them a certain percentage of the equity. Now I can do that as CEO of the company, but imagine if I tell my shareholders I am going to build a second factory in that country. I would get laughed out of the board room, right?

This message, I think you and I are in violent agreement here, any time I can help you make that pitch because that will attract investment because there is a lot of good about these areas in terms of investment prospects as well I think. Thank you.

Mr. SMITH. Thank you so very much for your testimony, your leadership, and look forward to working with you going forward. The hearing is adjourned.

[Whereupon, at 3:33 p.m., the subcommittee was adjourned.]

APPENDIX

MATERIAL SUBMITTED FOR THE RECORD

SUBCOMMITTEE HEARING NOTICE
COMMITTEE ON FOREIGN AFFAIRS
U.S. HOUSE OF REPRESENTATIVES
WASHINGTON, DC 20515-6128

Subcommittee on Africa, Global Health, Global Human Rights, and International Organizations
Christopher H. Smith (R-NJ), Chairman

October 22, 2015

TO: MEMBERS OF THE COMMITTEE ON FOREIGN AFFAIRS

You are respectfully requested to attend an OPEN hearing of the Committee on Foreign Affairs, to be held by the Subcommittee on Africa, Global Health, Global Human Rights, and International Organizations in Room 2200 of the Rayburn House Office Building (and available live on the Committee website at http://www.ForeignAffairs.house.gov):

DATE: Thursday, October 22, 2015

TIME: 2:00 p.m.

SUBJECT: Africa's Great Lakes Region: A Security, Political, and Humanitarian Challenge

WITNESSES: The Honorable Linda Thomas–Greenfield
Assistant Secretary
Bureau of African Affairs
U.S. Department of State

The Honorable Thomas Perriello
Special Envoy for the Great Lakes Region of Africa
U.S. Department of State

By Direction of the Chairman

COMMITTEE ON FOREIGN AFFAIRS

MINUTES OF SUBCOMMITTEE ON _Africa, Global Health, Global Human Rights, and International Organizations_ HEARING

Day _Thursday_ Date _October 22, 2015_ Room _2200 Rayburn HOB_

Starting Time _2:03 p.m._ Ending Time _3:33 p.m._

Recesses | _0_ | (___ to ___) (___ to ___) (___ to ___) (___ to ___) (___ to ___) (___ to ___)

Presiding Member(s)

Rep. Chris Smith

Check all of the following that apply:

Open Session ✓   Electronically Recorded (taped) ✓
Executive (closed) Session ☐   Stenographic Record ✓
Televised ✓

TITLE OF HEARING:

Africa's Great Lakes Region: A Security, Political, and Humanitarian Challenge

SUBCOMMITTEE MEMBERS PRESENT:

Rep. Mark Meadows, Rep. David Cicilline, Rep. Karen Bass, Rep. Curt Clawson

NON-SUBCOMMITTEE MEMBERS PRESENT: _(Mark with an * if they are not members of full committee.)_

HEARING WITNESSES: Same as meeting notice attached? Yes ✓ No ☐
(If "no", please list below and include title, agency, department, or organization.)

STATEMENTS FOR THE RECORD: _(List any statements submitted for the record.)_

TIME SCHEDULED TO RECONVENE _____
or
TIME ADJOURNED _3:33 p.m._

Gregory B. Simpkins
Subcommittee Staff Director